Oliver and Boyd Geography

Key Stage 2

Teacher's Book 1

David Flint

Acknowledgements

We are grateful to the following for permission to reproduce copyright material:

The National Council for Education Technology for an adapted extract from *Focus on IT*, © Crown Copyright 1991.

Cover photos by:

British Coal *(above right)*; Mark Edwards/Still Pictures *(below)*;
© John Harris *(above left)*.

Oliver & Boyd
Longman House,
Burnt Mill,
Harlow,
Essex,
CM20 2JE

An imprint of Longman Group UK Ltd.
© Oliver & Boyd 1992

All rights reserved; no part of this publication may be reproduced, stored in a retrieval system, or transmitted in any form or by any means, electronic, mechanical, photocopying, recording, or otherwise, without the prior written permission of the Publishers or a licence permitting restricted copying in the United Kingdom issued by the Copyright Licensing Agency Ltd, 90 Tottenham Court Road, London, W1P 9HE.

ISBN 0 05 004598 9

First published 1992

Set in 10/12pt New Century Schoolbook (Linotron)

Printed in Great Britain
by the Bath Press

The publisher's policy is to use paper manufactured from sustainable forests.

Designed by Marcus Askwith

Contents

		Page
Section 1:	Introducing Oliver and Boyd Geography	5
	Introduction	7
	Oliver and Boyd Geography: Key Stage 2 materials	8
	The components	8
	Using the Key Stage 2 materials	9
	Pupil Books	9
	Copymasters	10
	Teacher's Books	11
	Using Pupil Book 1, Copymasters 1 and Teacher's Book 1	12
	Using Oliver and Boyd Geography to plan a unit of work on Mining and Quarrying	13
	Matrices showing coverage of Statements of Attainment	15
	Pupil Book 1	15
	Copymasters 1	16
	Progression Pathways: Selected Strands from Attainment Targets	18
Section 2:	**Using Oliver and Boyd Geography**	19
	Pupil Book 1 Contents	20
	In the Neighbourhood	21
	1 A neighbourhood in Inverness	22
	2 A neighbourhood in Coventry	28
	Quarries and Mines	34
	3 Slate from North Wales	35
	4 Coal mining in Yorkshire	42
	People on the Move	49
	5 Moving to the coast: Southport	50
	6 On the move in the Sahel	55
Section 3:	**Oliver and Boyd Geography and the National Curriculum**	69
	Geography at Key Stage 2	70
	Programme of Study for Key Stage 2	71
	What do the Statutory Orders mean?	76
	Where does geography fit in the school curriculum?	78
	What should teachers be trying to do in geography at Key Stage 2?	78
	Developing mapwork skills using Oliver and Boyd Geography	80
	Using photographs in Oliver and Boyd Geography	82
	Planning work with a geographical content	84
	Good practice	84
Section 4:	**Assessment, Recording, Cross-curricular elements and Information Technology (IT)**	87
	Assessing and recording pupil progress	88
	What should an eleven-year-old be able to do in geography?	88
	Recording pupil progress	89
	A sample class record sheet for Key Stage 2	91
	Curriculum mapping	92
	Record of Achievement sample sheets	93
	Cross-curricular elements	95
	Cross-curricular themes	95
	Cross-curricular dimensions	99
	Cross-curricular skills	99

	Information Technology (IT)	100
	Introduction	100
	Communicating information	100
	Handling information	101
	Modelling	102
	Measurement and control	102
	Evaluating applications and effects	103
Section 5:	**Implementing National Curriculum Geography at Key Stage 2: developing school-based INSET**	105
	Introduction	106
	The role of the geography co-ordinator	106
	Planning school-based INSET: some key questions	107
	Managing curriculum change	108
	Where are we now?	108
	Where do we want to be?	108
	How are we going to achieve what we want?	109
	Planning a Key Stage 2 programme	109
	Planning a unit of work based on key questions	110
	Assessment in geography	113
	Assessment checklist	113
	Fieldwork in geography at Key Stage 2	114
	Appendices	116
	1 Geography resource checklist	116
	2 Story and poetry books	118
	3 Useful addresses	119
	4 Useful addresses (Geographical resources and support)	120

Section 1:

Introducing Oliver and Boyd Geography

Introduction

Oliver and Boyd Geography is a range of resources specifically written to introduce children to geography at Key Stages 1 and 2. Whilst the starting point for creating the materials was the National Curriculum – and specifically the Statutory Orders for Geography – the authors were at the same time guided by their own views and experience of what constitutes good geography and good primary practice.

Approaches to teaching geography at Key Stage 2 appear to fall into two broad categories. Some schools have chosen a cross-curricular approach to topics and themes. In these cases, geographical knowledge, skills and ideas are developed in the context of broad topics which may also include aspects of history, science, English, mathematics and art. Other schools have chosen to identify geography as a separate element of the timetable in order to develop the subject's particular body of knowledge, skills and ideas in a more focused and compartmentalised way.

The authors make no judgements about the relative merits of each of these approaches. In planning *Oliver and Boyd Geography*, they were aware that such variety in teaching approaches exists and that published materials should leave teachers free to follow their own line of approach. The Pupil Books contain an average of nine units, collected together into two or three sections, each section being devoted to one theme. Thus, depending on their chosen method of approach, teachers can teach one section per term or extract individual units to fit into an integrated cross-curricular programme. This format of the Pupil Books, plus the linked Copymasters and Teacher's Books, should provide the support, the flexibility and the range of choice that the busy teacher needs.

Oliver and Boyd Geography: Key Stage 2 materials

The components

There are three main components in the Key Stage 2 materials.

Pupil Books

There are five books which cover the four years of Key Stage 2.

The selection of material for each book was governed by both the Programmes of Study and by Attainment Targets for levels 2-5. Thus there is a gradual progression from Book 1 to Book 5. Each book focuses on two levels, but with one more dominant than the other (see contents list below).

The progression in content and level of difficulty from one book to another is evident in their presentation. In particular, the change in the style and complexity of the maps reflects the need for progressive development in map reading skills. The length of the books also increases to encompass the expanding content load of the curriculum. Language levels and type sizes, etc., have also been carefully graded from Book 1 to Book 5.

There are sets of questions and activities at the end of most double-page spreads which encourage pupils to focus on the key ideas underlying the text and illustrations, and to develop and practise map reading and photo interpretation skills (see pages 80–83).

Each book is divided into three main sections (see list below), which are in turn broken down into two or three units. A full list of Contents for Book 1 is given in Section 2, page 20.

Book 1 (Levels 2/**3**)
In the Neighbourhood
Quarries and Mines
People on the Move

Book 2 (Levels **3**/4)
Farming in Britain
Settlements
Going Places

Book 3 (Levels 3/**4**)
Farming at Home and Abroad
Trade and Industry
Rivers and Lakes

Book 4 (Levels **4**/5)
Shaping the Landscape
Communications
Inside Big Cities

Book 5 (Levels 4/**5**)
Places and People
People and Environments

Copymasters

There are five sets of Copymasters, one to link with each of the five Pupil Books. These are designed to be photocopied for use by the pupils, and each pack contains guidance for the teacher on ways of using the resources. A Contents list for Copymaster Set 1 (to link with Pupil Book 1) is given on page 11.

Teacher's Books

There are five Teacher's Books, one linked to each Pupil Book and Copymaster set (see page 12).

Using the Key Stage 2 materials

Pupil Books

Taken together the five books (and related Copymasters) provide a good coverage of the Programme of Study for Key Stage 2, as well as the Statements of Attainment.

Each book contains studies set in localities drawn from the UK, economically developing countries and economically developed countries (including the EC).

The structure of Books 1 to 4 comprises three sections, defined by one main theme. Each one is divided into two or three units, which in turn are broken down into sub-units. The main sections should provide a content load for a term's work (if taken together with the linked Copymasters), assuming teachers are following a broadly linear pattern of teaching, with a subject focus. Book 5 has only two sections, each comprising several discrete units, and is not organised on a termly basis.

There is a dominant focus in each book, both in terms of level and themes, but each one overlaps with the ones before and the ones after. (See matrix on page 18). Thus, Book 1 focuses on levels 2/3 and revisits and extends the coverage of themes which were introduced in the later Key Stage 1 books (e.g. journeys, homes, routes, transport and work). Books 2 and 3 focus on levels 3/4 and Books 4 and 5 move towards levels 4/5.

For all the books, the authors have researched their own materials, using real people as the focus of many of the studies, thus providing a 'familiar' feel to the material. The extensive use – especially in the early books – of photographs (many taken specially), pictorial maps, sketches and other maps also helps vividly to emphasise the 'reality' of the more distant localities, as well as providing a thoroughly stimulating visual impression. The books serve to bring the world into the classroom and in the case of the localities studied can be seen as simulated fieldwork based on indirect observation.

- The early books have a predominance of topics and localities within the UK, i.e. closest to the children's direct experience. However, following Book 1 there is a growing number of locality studies set in more 'distant' places, especially economically developing countries, in order to ensure the breadth of vision and balance so vital to geography at Key Stage 2. These early books also revisit some of the ideas and places introduced in the Key Stage 1 books, e.g. the journey to school, and the locality of Edgwick in Coventry.

- In the later books the key ideas and skills introduced in the earlier books are further developed in the context of more unfamiliar, distant places. In addition the range of geographical material widens to include further aspects of industry, transport, settlement, population, weather, rivers, landforms, soil and resources.

- Each section in each of the five books comprises two or three units which provide a web of interrelated topics and ideas linked to one dominant theme. Thus, in Book 1, in the first section called *In the Neighbourhood*, children will encounter a wide range of geographical ideas and topics, such as house types, shops, transport, and change over time, in the context of actual localities, i.e. Inverness and Coventry. Teachers are therefore free to select and highlight different strands (e.g. housing) as appropriate to their chosen course of study.

The units in each book can be introduced and used in different ways:
- as stimuli or exemplars for class or group discussion about the pupils' own experiences (e.g. *In the Neighbourhood*, and *People on the Move*, in Book 1, and *Settlements* in Book 2.);

- as sources of information which pupils can refer to in connection with a class or group activity such as 'Weather';
- as resources to be used selectively in the context of wider cross-curricular themes (e.g. *Quarries and Mines* in Book 1 can contribute to the theme of environmental education);
- as the basis (taken together with the Copymasters) for teaching geographical skills;
- as the basis for the study of actual places (e.g. the Sahel, North Wales, Almere in The Netherlands);
- to form the basis for topic work on, for example, houses and homes (e.g. *In the Neighbourhood* in Book 1).

Order of use

The authors do not prescribe that teachers should use Pupil Book 1 with year 3, and Pupil Book 2 with year 4 pupils in a strict sequence. Nevertheless, in writing the books, the authors were careful to introduce a clear progression, in terms of skills, knowledge and understanding, from Book 1 to Book 5. There is also an increase in the volume and depth of the material between Book 1 and Book 5. The authors take the view that it is vital to introduce some 'distant place' material at an early stage, and to continue this in each book. Thus, such material was introduced in the later Key Stage 1 materials, and appears in each of the five Key Stage 2 books.

Copymasters

The Copymasters provide activities for children which will develop geographical skills, knowledge and understanding appropriate to levels 2 to 5 in the Statutory Orders.

The activities in the Copymasters are designed to reinforce and develop key ideas and skills introduced in the Pupil Books. The majority of activities are closely linked to a particular unit or resource in the Pupil Books. It is vital, therefore, that these materials are given to the pupils at the point when they are using the relevant Pupil Book material (e.g. photographs, maps, and diagrams).

The Copymasters can be used as assessment items, and have an important diagnostic function in relation to identifying pupil progress. As the matrix on pages 16 and 17 shows, most Copymaster activities relate to specific Statements of Attainment within the Statutory Orders for Geography, but many also relate to the Programme of Study or to general geographical skills and content not specifically mentioned in the Orders.

The sequence of the Copymasters matches that of the Pupil Books and there is a clear progression in terms of skills, knowledge and ideas.

Most of the Copymasters have been designed so that children can work on them independently, or at least with minimal help. Children who have reading difficulties may need help with the written instructions, but these have been written as simply and explicitly as possible so that able readers can work through them on their own.

Some of the Copymasters carry no written instructions. This is because space did not allow it, and because the instructions would be too lengthy or complex for the children to follow. Suggestions for their use, including different approaches, are detailed on the introductory card in each Copymaster pack.

There are also some Copymasters which introduce ideas not explicitly covered in the related Pupil Book (e.g. in Set 1 Copymaster 43 *Why move to*

Southport? and 53 *Moving from country to town*). These masters are intended to extend the range and depth of coverage of the topics from the Pupil Books.

The authors realise that within a given group of children there may be a wide variation in levels of achievement. The Copymasters are designed to cater for this range of achievement, either by providing reinforcement and practice material for less successful pupils, or by providing extension material to stretch the more able.

Teacher's Books

The primary purpose of these five books is to provide a commentary on each of the *Oliver and Boyd Geography* Pupil Books at Key Stage 2. They are also designed to serve a wider purpose, namely to assist teachers who may be unfamiliar with the new curriculum or with geographical work. For example, in Section 2, geographical background information is provided in relation to each unit in the relevant Pupil Book. This has been compiled with non-specialist teachers in mind, who may feel the need for support in terms of factual information which is presented at their own level, and who may lack confidence when teaching certain geographical topics for the first time. Thus, for the unit on the Sahel in Book 1, the 'background information' section provides factual information on desertification and statistical material comparing Burkina Faso with the UK. Similarly, for the unit on Eurotunnel in Book 2, up-to-date facts are given in Section 2 of Teacher's Book 2.

Each Teacher's Book is divided into five sections:

Section 1: Introducing Oliver and Boyd Geography describes the basic components of the publication, its broad aims and links with the Statutory Orders for Geography.

Section 2: Using Oliver and Boyd Geography materials
This section examines the relevant Pupil Book in depth, taking each unit in turn. It opens with a summary of the content and purpose of each unit, then gives background information relevant to the key topic of each unit. This is followed by a checklist of key ideas. Questions for discussion with the pupils are followed by notes on the links between the Pupil Book material and related Copymasters, and each sub-section ends with a list of suggested further activities to develop and enhance the pupils' grasp of geographical skills, ideas and knowledge. Relevant geography ATs are listed next to each activity.

Section 3: Oliver and Boyd Geography and the National Curriculum opens with a straightforward summary and analysis of the Statutory Orders for Geography, and offers guidance and suggestions for ways in which teachers can develop geographical work at Key Stage 2. The National Curriculum Council (NCC) and the Curriculum Council for Wales (CCW) Geography Non-Statutory Guidance documents also provide useful support. This section also includes notes on enquiry, and on values and attitudes in geography, plus checklists on mapwork skills and photographs in relation to *Oliver and Boyd Geography*.

Section 4: Assessment, Recording, Cross-curricular elements and Information Technology (IT)
The specific help offered by *Oliver and Boyd Geography* in relation to these topics is spelt out in depth in this section.

Section 5: Implementing National Curriculum Geography at Key Stage 2: developing school-based INSET provides some ideas for running INSET sessions on implementing the National Curriculum for Geography, using *Oliver and Boyd Geography*. It includes a sub-section on planning a unit of work based on a topic drawn from the related Pupil Book. The section ends with practical ideas for fieldwork – a vital element in geographical work at Key Stage 2.

Oliver & Boyd Geography Teacher's Book 1

Appendices
There are at least three of these in each Teacher's Book:

Geography Resource Checklist
Useful Addresses (IT)
Useful Addresses (Geographical resources and support)

This Teacher's Book 1, as with Key Stage 1 Teacher's Book, also includes an Appendix which lists story books appropriate for use with young children in relation to geographical work.

Using Pupil Book 1, Copymasters 1 and Teacher's Book 1

Section 2 in this Teacher's Book provides a detailed breakdown of Pupil Book 1, together with numerous suggestions for activities which link to its content and which will develop and extend the children's work in directions selected by the teacher. Section 2 also shows how Book 1 can be linked with Copymasters 1 to provide support and extension as well as the basis for assessment and recording pupils' progress and understanding. (See also the matrix on page 15 showing the coverage of the Statements of Attainment within Pupil Book 1.)

Copymasters 1

In the following Contents list, the Copymasters are grouped under the unit and sub-unit headings to which they relate in Pupil Book 1.

In the Neighbourhood
A neighbourhood in Inverness
1 Building materials
2 Different types of homes
3 Plans
4 More plans
5 A plan of Emily's bedroom
6 A plan of Jo's living room
7 Routes round Jo's living room
8 Simon's bedroom
9 Symbols and messages
10 Garden plan
11 Inverness neighbourhood
12 Simon's Monday
13 My day
14 Shops in Inverness
15 Routes around a school
16 Around Crown School
17 Shops

A neighbourhood in Coventry
18 The Blackwell Road area
19 Making up symbols
20 People in the street
21 Changes around Blackwell Road
22 An industrial estate
23 Changes in Foleshill Road
24 Shops in Foleshill Road

Quarries and Mines
Slate from North Wales
25 Around Blaenau Ffestiniog
26 Living near a quarry
27 Llechwedd Slate Caverns
28 A gravel pit
29 A slate town in North Wales

30 The Ffestiniog Railway
31 Moving around
32 Blaenau Ffestiniog from above

Coal mining in Yorkshire
33 Opencast coal mining
34 Britain's coalfields
35 An old coal mine
36 A miner's day in 1920
37 A miner's day in 1990
38 An opencast coal mine
39 Coal mining today
40 The Selby Coalfield
41 Coal mining in the Selby area
42 Changes in a mining area

People on the Move
Moving to the coast: Southport
43 Why move to Southport?
44 Southport's sea front
45 Southport from above
46 Using Southport's parks
47 In the park

On the move in the Sahel
48 Africa
49 A village in Burkina Faso
50 The magic stones
51 Water in Burkina Faso
52 A woman's work
53 Moving from country to town
54 Abidjan

55 The British Isles
56 Europe
57 The World

Introducing Oliver & Boyd Geography

> Using *Oliver and Boyd Geography* to plan a unit of work on Mining and Quarrying

The following is a suggested sequence of activities that teachers might follow in planning a unit of work on a given topic. The topic chosen here is 'Mining and Quarrying' for which there are two studies in Pupil Book 1. The sequence is designed to show how *Oliver and Boyd Geography* links to the National Curriculum, and how the different elements within the publication are mutually reinforcing.

Sequence

Identify key statements from the Key Stage 2 Programme of Study for Geography (see page 71).

Environmental Geography – Pupils should be taught:
- ways of extracting materials from the environment and how the extraction of natural resources affects environments, for example quarries, mining;
- ways in which people look after and improve the environment; some of the ways in which damaged environments can be restored and damage prevented; and to consider whether some types of environment need special protection.

Geographical skills – Pupils should be taught to:
- use pictures and photographs to identify features, for example homes, railways, rivers, hills, and to find out about places; describe what they see using geographical terms.

↓

Refer to *Oliver and Boyd Geography* Key Stage 1 Teacher's Book, then identify the key questions about mining and quarrying, which will form the basis for the study, e.g.

(a) What do the children already know about mining and quarrying?

(b) What are the differences between mining and quarrying?

(c) Why are mining and quarrying important?

(d) What are the main products of mining and quarrying?

(e) Which places in Britain are involved in mining and quarrying?

(f) How have mining and quarrying changed?

(g) What are the effects of mining and quarrying on the landscape?

(h) How can areas be restored after mining and quarrying?

↓

Decide on whether the topic will address some or all of the above questions.
Examine links with science, technology, history and cross-curricular links such as economic awareness, environmental education and other curriculum areas (refer to *Oliver and Boyd Geography*, Key Stage 1 Teacher's Book) and add additional activities (see Further Activities in Section 2 of this Teacher's Book) with particular reference to IT.

↓

Refer to Pupil Book 1

- Identify which units or sub-units of the book relate to key ideas. E.g. 'Slate all around' (pages 40 and 41) links to the effects of quarrying on the landscape.
- Refer to Teacher's Book for additional background information.
- Refer to *Oliver and Boyd Geography* Key Stage 1 Teacher's Book for questions to ask the children at each stage of the learning process. Build these into the teaching scheme.

⬇

Refer to Copymasters 1 for related activities:

Copymaster numbers
26 Living near a quarry
27 Llechwedd slate caverns
28 A gravel pit
29 A slate town in North Wales
30 The Ffestiniog Railway
31 Moving around
32 Blaenau Ffestiniog from above
33 Opencast coal mining
34 Britain's Coalfields
35 An old coal mine
36 A miner's day in 1920
37 A miner's day in 1990
38 An opencast coal mine
39 Coal mining today
40 The Selby Coalfield
41 Coal mining in the Selby area
42 Changes in a mining area

Some Copymasters may form the basis of core activities for all children, e.g. 26, 28, 32, 33, 38, 39, 42. Others may form the basis of extension activities for different groups, e.g. 27, 30, 31, 34, 35, 36, 37, 40, 41. These can now be incorporated into the teaching scheme.

⬇

Refer to Teacher's Book 1 and consider evaluation and assessment in relation to the theme. Which activities could form the basis for suitable pieces of assessment? For example, identifying the main differences between mining and quarrying; listing the main effects of quarrying on the environment.

⬇

Make final decisions about the nature, sequence and structure of the teaching scheme and where the different elements of *Oliver and Boyd Geography* will be used.

Introducing Oliver & Boyd Geography

Coverage of Statements of Attainment in Pupil Book 1

Key Stage 2 Pupil Book 1 / Geography Attainment Targets	In the Neighbourhood — A neighbourhood in Inverness	In the Neighbourhood — A neighbourhood in Coventry	Quarries and Mines — Slate from North Wales	Quarries and Mines — Coal mining in Yorkshire	People on the Move — Moving to the coast: Southport	People on the Move — On the move in the Sahel
AT1 Skills	2c, 2e 3b, 3c	2c, 2e 3a, 3b, 3c, 3d	2a, 2e 3a, 3d	2a, 2e 3a, 3d	2a, 2e 3a, 3d	2a, 2e 3d
AT2 Places	2b, 2c 3c, 3e, 3f	2b 3c, 3e, 3f	3c, 3e, 3f	3c, 3e, 3f	3e, 3f	2c, 2d 3d
AT3 Physical Geography						2b 3a
AT4 Human Geography	2a, 2b, 2c 3d	2a, 2b, 2c 3b, 3d	3b, 3c, 3d	3c, 3d	2b, 2c 3a, 3b, 3c, 3d	2b, 2c 3a, 3d
AT5 Environmental Geography		2b	2a, 2b 3a	2a, 2b 3a		2b

Coverage of Statements of Attainment in Copymasters 1

Levels 2/3	AT1									AT2										AT3							AT4							AT5				
Copymasters	2a	2b	2c	2d	2e	3a	3b	3c	3d	2a	2b	2c	2d	3a	3b	3c	3d	3e	3f	2a	2b	3a	3b	3c	2a	2b	2c	3a	3b	3c	3d	2a	2b	2c	3a	3b
1											X																										
2											X										X																
3																																					
4																																					
5			●																																		
6																																					
7			●																																		
8																																					
9																																					
10											X																										
11						●																															
12																																					
13											X																										
14																											●										
15			●								X																										
16			●																																		
17											X																	●									
18							●																														
19																																					
20																												●									
21					●																												●				
22											X																●										
23								X																			●										
24											X																										
25										●	X																										
26											X																						●				
27			●					X																									X		●	●	
28																																	X	X	●		
29											X																										
30			●																																		
31																														●							
32									●																				X				X		●	●	
33									X																							X					
34																																					
35																															X		X			X	
36																																●					

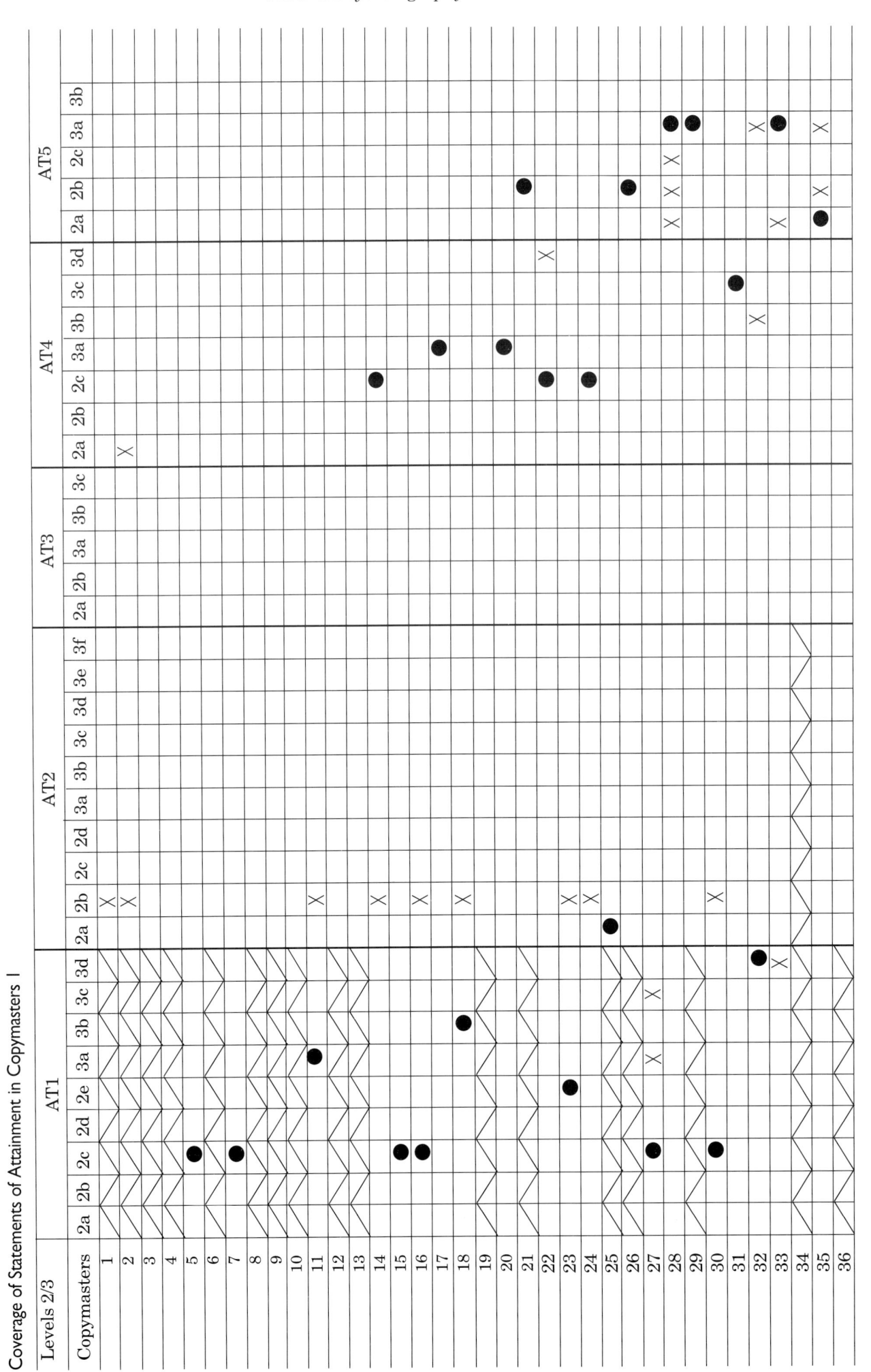

Introducing Oliver & Boyd Geography

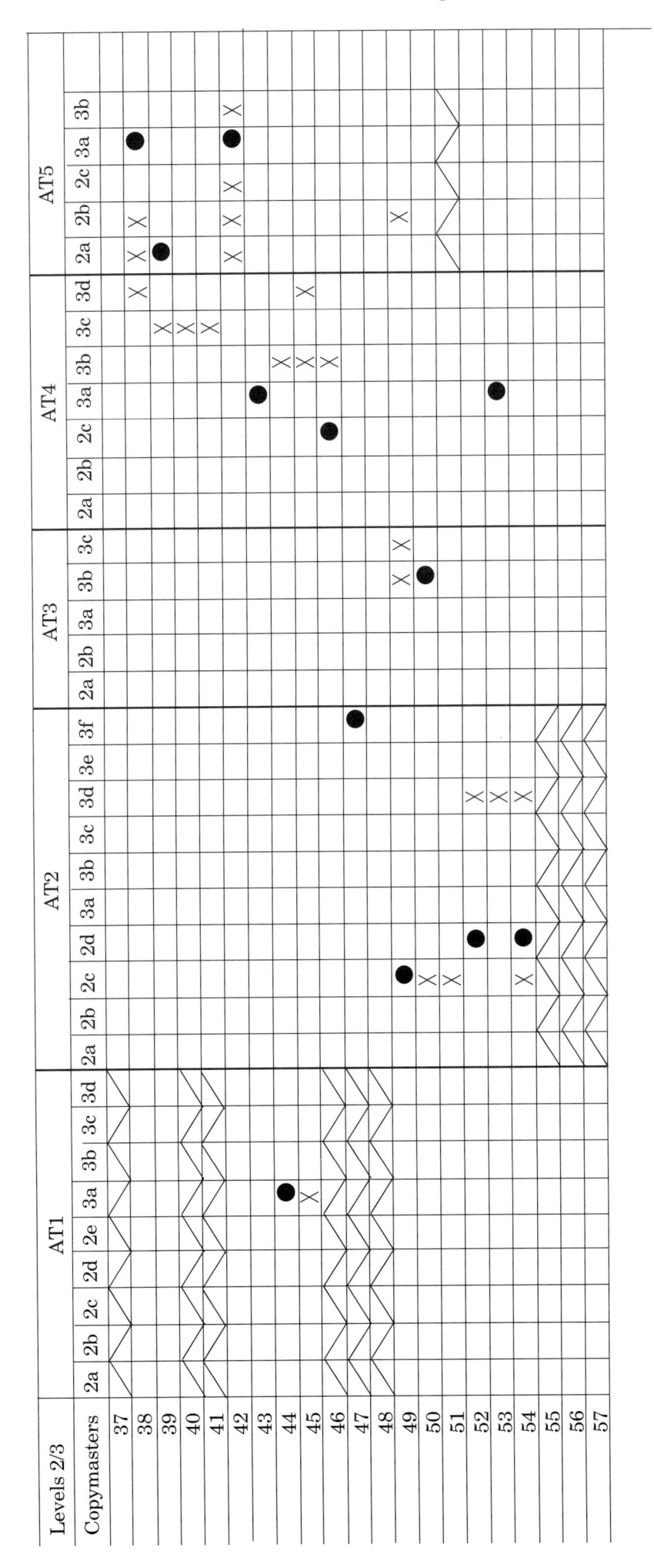

Levels 2/3	AT1								AT2										AT3						AT4						AT5				
Copymasters	2a	2b	2c	2d	2e	3a	3b	3c	3d	2a	2b	2c	2d	3a	3b	3c	3d	3e	3f	2a	2b	3a	3b	3c	2a	2b	2c	3a	3b	3c	3d	2a	2b	2c	3a	3b
37																																			●	
38																																X	X			
39																																●				
40																																				
41																																				
42																																X	X	X	●	X
43																																				
44						●																						●								
45						X																					●		X							
46																													X	X						
47																			●				X	X						X					
48																																				
49												●																								
50												X				X	X	X																		
51												X																								
52													●																							
53													●																							
54												X																					X			
55																																				
56																																				
57																																				

● The main SoA covered

X Subsidiary SoA's covered

⋀ The main AT to which the activity relates

(Note: Some activities relate to the Programme of Study or to geographical skills/content not specifically mentioned in the Statutory Orders, hence the coding under AT rather than SoA.)

17

Progression Pathways: Selected Strands from Attainment Targets

	Key Stage 1 Materials	Key Stage 2 Book 1	Key Stage 2 Book 2

STRANDS

Use of Maps

AT1	Going to School Living in a Village Living in a City	← {	Inverness Coventry (Edgwick) Southport	} →	Newport Le Puy Delhi

Localities

AT2	Going to School Living in a Village Living in a City Living in Hong Kong	← {	Southport Burkina Faso (village) Ivory Coast (Abidjan)	} →	Newport Le Puy Delhi

Weather

AT3	Weather In the Mountains Cold Places Hot Places	← {	Southport Burkina Faso	} →	Weather and the Farmer

Settlements

AT4	Living in a Village Living in a City Days Out Living in Hong Kong	← {	Blaenau Ffestiniog (quarries and mines) Southport Ivory Coast (Abidjan) Burkina Faso (village)	} →	Newport Le Puy Delhi

Movement

AT4	Going to School Days Out Hot Places Living on Islands	← {	Southport Burkina Faso	} →	Panama Canal Peru Eurotunnel

Economic Activity

AT4 AT5	Living on Islands Cold Places Hot Places	← {	Inverness Coventry (Edgwick) Slate (quarries and mines) Coal	} →	Farming (Lake District) Farming (East Anglia) Eurotunnel

See Statutory Orders for Geography for a complete list of Strands within each Attainment Target.

Section 2:

Using Oliver and Boyd Geography

Pupil Book 1 Contents

In the Neighbourhood

1 A neighbourhood in Inverness   2
    The route to school   2
    Houses near Crown School   8
    The local shopping centre   10
    A busy corner   14

2 A neighbourhood in Coventry   16
    Home and school   16
    Changes in the Blackwell Road area   18
    Changes near Edgewick School   22
    Change in Foleshill Road   26

Quarries and Mines

3 Slate from North Wales   30
    Slate and its uses   30
    The old slate mines   32
    Slate quarrying today   36
    Tourists come to Llechwedd   38
    Slate all around   40

4 Coal mining in Yorkshire   42
    Coal and its uses   42
    Opencast mining   43
    Coal under Yorkshire   44
    The work of the miners   46
    From coal to electricity   49
    Changes in mining   50

People on the Move

5 Moving to the coast: Southport   54
    Welcome to Southport!   54
    Homes for old people in Southport   56
    Southport in the past   58
    Moving around in Southport   62

6 On the move in the Sahel   64
    A village in Burkina Faso   64
    Finding food   66
    The magic stones   70
    The firewood and water trail   72
    Finding work   76

In the Neighbourhood

1 A neighbourhood in Inverness
   The route to school
   Houses near Crown School
   The local shopping centre
   A busy corner

2 A neighbourhood in Coventry
   Home and school
   Changes in the Blackwell Road area
   Changes near Edgewick School
   Changes in Foleshill Road

A neighbourhood in Inverness

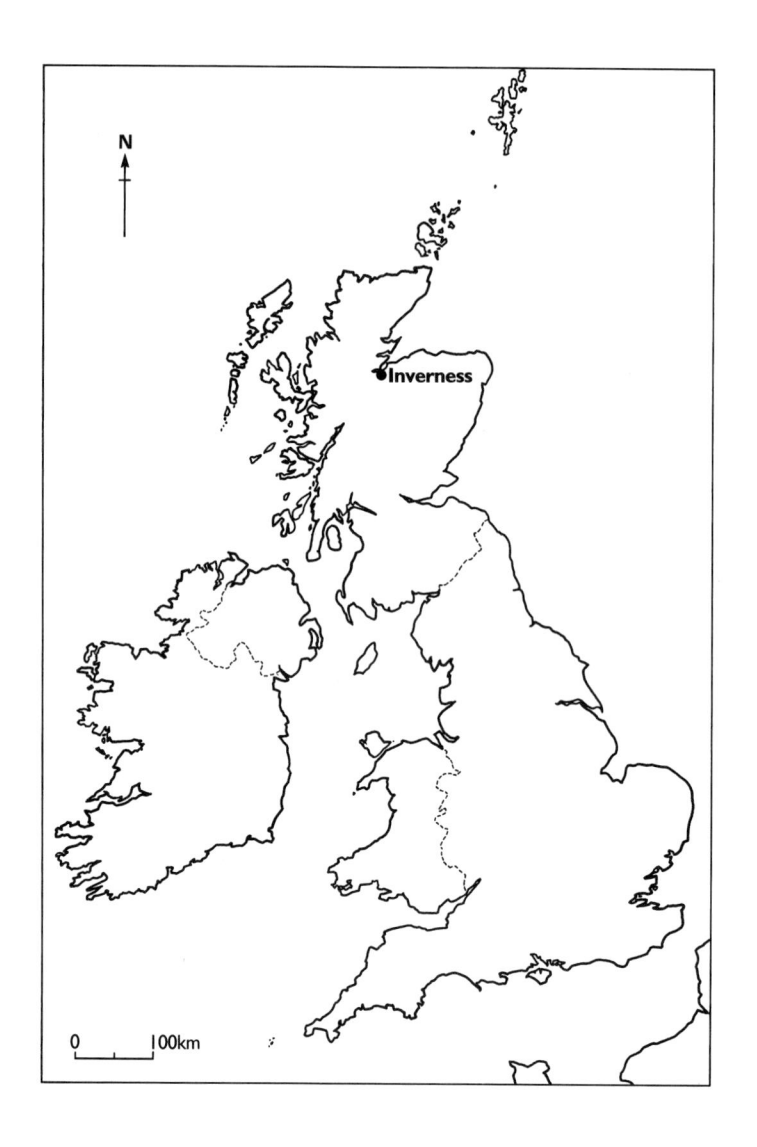

Related Copymasters 1-17	**Main Attainment Target**	AT2 Knowledge and Understanding of Places
	Key Statements of Attainment	*describe uses of land and buildings in the local area (AT2/2b)*
		identify features of a locality outside the local area and suggest how these might affect the lives of people who live there (AT2/2c)
	Other relevant Statements of Attainment	AT1/2c, 2e, 3b, 3c AT2/3c, 3e, 3f AT4/2a, 2b, 2c, 3d

(Links between this unit, the Key Stage 1 Pupil Books and Book 2 are shown in the matrix on page 18 of this book.)

1 Summary and purpose

The unit as a whole

'A locality should be a small area with distinctive features, and in the case of the local area is the immediate vicinity of the school or where the pupil lives.' (Programme of Study for Key Stage 1)

The purpose of this unit is to provide a detailed case study of a UK locality - in this case, the local area of a school. This is the type of study which could form the basis for similar work by all pupils in their own localities. It focuses on real children in a real situation, and can provide detail for comparisons highlighting both similarities and differences.

Further, this unit returns to themes first developed in the Key Stage 1 Pupil Books *Going to School*, *Living in a Village*, and *Living in a City*. The intention is to develop and extend specific key ideas such as routes; for example routes from home to school, and routes to the local shops. Other key ideas relate to houses and house types, as well as shops and shopping. In this way the series ensures a progressive development of key ideas, knowledge and understanding.

Sub-units

The route to school details the route from home to school followed in Inverness by Emily and Simon, two characters from the Key Stage 1 materials. Emily's own description of the route identifies key landmarks such as the traffic lights and the church. Virtually all pupils will share a similar experience of a journey to school, and this spread can form the basis for comparisons as well as activities such as writing descriptions similar to Emily's. In the same way the map of the route provides a useful model which teachers may wish their pupils to emulate. These activities involving map reading and map drawing skills form one of the key elements of progression in the series. At Key Stage 1 pupils identified scenes along their route to school, and carried out simple activities such as sequencing such scenes or drawing picture maps of the route. This Pupil Book uses the same idea, but now the emphasis is on drawing more accurate and refined maps, which incorporate ideas about plan views as well as routes and key landmarks. In this way pupils' geographical skills are both extended and refined.

The use of two-dimensional map symbols, a compass and a key is introduced here for the first time, so marks a transition from the pictorial treatment in the Key Stage 1 materials to the more formal and symbolic style.

Houses near Crown School focuses on different house types in the area near Emily and Simon's school. Three different types of house are illustrated (by photographs) and are also shown in plan view and on a map of the school neighbourhood. The material could form a model for similar work by children in other parts of the UK. The idea of maps which use plan view, directions and a key is further developed.

The local shopping centre Shops are an important part of locality studies, particularly in urban areas. This section uses a child-drawn map plus photographs to illustrate the type and location of shops near Crown School, Inverness. Specific shops are then shown in greater detail so that pupils can identify their contents. The shopping list activity is one which can be matched in most UK localities.

A busy corner focuses on a major crossing point near Crown School and so serves as a useful introduction to ideas about road safety, specifically crossing roads safely, which could form the basis for further work, including cross-curricular work.

2 Background information

This area of Inverness has many features typical of nineteenth-century suburban localities elsewhere in the UK, such as:

- schools;
- different types of housing (semi-detached, detached, terraced, mostly with gardens);
- different ages of housing (mostly nineteenth-century to modern);
- a local shopping centre with a few shops meeting very 'local' needs, i.e. newsagent, post office, greengrocer;
- road junctions busy with traffic (mostly cars, buses and bicycles).

Where Inverness is less typical is in the extensive use of local stone in houses, streets and gardens. In other parts of the UK, limestone, granite, slate, chalk or sandstone are used in similar ways and useful comparisons can be drawn. Elsewhere, brick and tile are the more usual building materials and again fruitful comparisons can be made.

Similarly, some UK towns will have shops developed in converted houses, as in the case of Inverness, whilst others will have purpose-built suburban shops. The number, size and nature of the Inverness shops can be directly compared with shops in the pupils' own localities.

The cluster of shops in this Pupil Book shows a typical location around a road junction. The attraction of such junctions in terms of generating customers (linked to converging bus routes) can usefully be explored with the children, and is a good example for AT2/3f which requires an explanation of the location of key features such as shops within the local area. Safety issues relating to the junction can also be explored.

3 Key ideas

1. Maps show where places are.
2. Maps help us find our way from place to place.
3. There are key landmarks such as buildings and busy road junctions along the journey to school.
4. Different building materials are used for different parts of schools, houses and shops.
5. The journey from home to school can be long or short (in both distance and time).
6. Houses can be changed over time into other uses, e.g. an hotel, a doctor's surgery.
7. There are hazards to be faced on the way to school, such as crossing busy roads.
8. Some pedestrian crossings are controlled by traffic lights.
9. There are terraced, semi-detached and detached houses near Crown School.
10. Many houses have gardens.
11. Local shopping centres have few shops.
12. Local shopping centres often grow up at road junctions.

13 Local shopping centres sell goods which meet people's short-term needs.
14 Streets near shops are busy with traffic.
15 Late afternoon (when children come out of school) is a busy time in the streets around schools.

4 Questions for discussion with the children

The route to school

Where – is Crown School?

– does May live? (See Emily's description on page 3.)

– is the church?

What – time does Emily leave home?

– was the hotel in the past?

When – do Emily and May cross the road?

Houses near Crown School

Where – are Crown Street and Hill Street?

– are there detached houses?

What – are terraced houses?

– are semi-detached houses?

– are detached houses?

Which – houses have two storeys?

– houses have gardens?

The local shopping centre

Where – is the local shopping centre?

– do Emily and Simon cross the road?

What – shops are in this shopping centre?

– items do Emily and Simon have to buy?

Why – do Emily and Simon sometimes have to go to other shopping centres?

A busy corner

Where – are the streets busy?

– is the pub?

– is the chemist's shop?

What – time do children leave school?

Why – are the shops near where the roads meet?

How – do children cross the road safely?

– many roads meet near Crown school?

Oliver & Boyd Geography Teacher's Book 1

5 Links with Copymasters

Copymaster number and title	Main focus/purpose
1 Building materials	Identifies building materials
2 Different types of home	Identifies semi-detached, detached etc.
3 Plans	Introduces plan view for maps
4 More plans	Develops idea of plan view
5 A plan of Emily's bedroom	Links plan view with routes
6 A plan of Jo's living room	Links picture view and plan view
7 Routes round Jo's living room	Routes and plan view
8 Simon's bedroom	Links plan view with simple ideas of the scale of objects
9 Symbols and messages	Introduces the meaning and use of symbols
10 Garden plan	Develops the use of key symbols and plan view
11 Inverness neighbourhood	Work on letter-number coordinates
12 Simon's Monday	Interpreting data from pie graph
13 My day	Interpreting data from pie graph
14 Shops in Inverness	Linking shop usage and type
15 Routes around a school	Plan view with routes
16 Around Crown School	Adding items to maps
17 Shops	Classifying shops

6 Further activities

AT1/3c

1. Children can write their own descriptions of their routes to school, based on Emily's account on page 3.

AT1/3c, AT2/2b

2. Maps drawn by children of the area around the school can be used as a basis for drawing routes from home to school. More formal maps (similar to the one on pages 4 and 5) can also be used for this purpose, together with locating other key features of the local area (places of worship, garages, shops etc.).

AT4/2a

3. Children can annotate simple sketches of their own school or homes to identify the different building materials used. The properties of such materials can then be investigated, e.g. degree of waterproofing, hardness, ability to transmit heat. Further work could centre on the origin of particular building materials such as bricks, for example, where they come from and how they are made. Similar work could be pursued on concrete, slate (see pages 30-41 of the Pupil Book), tiles, timber and glass.

Using Oliver & Boyd Geography

AT2/2b	4	Large-scale maps and plans of the area around the school need careful introduction. Children should be introduced to them through studying a relatively small area, preferably one they can walk round with their teacher, annotating on a map the key points they visit, e.g. shops, houses, grass verges, bus stops. In this way teachers can help children make a direct link between what they see on the map and what they see on the ground. This activity also leads to the idea of using keys on maps to explain the meaning of the colours and symbols employed.
AT2/2b	5	A class can produce a map of the area around their own school, showing different house types, similar to that on pages 8-9. This can form a useful development from activities identifying the characteristics of different house types, and thus develop a sense of spatial awareness. It is important at this stage to keep maps simple and clear, showing individual houses, street names and the four main compass points.
AT2/2b, AT4/2c, AT1/3b	6	A survey of shops local to the school can lead to maps and 3D models showing shop locations in relation to main roads, and other landmarks such as pubs, places of worship and garages. Children can also allocate products from a list to the relevant shops which sell each item.
AT2/2b, AT4/2c	7	Children can design and make shop fronts, based on a local survey. They can then produce suitably priced items for each window.
AT4/2c	8	A simple census of local shops can reveal how many people use each shop over a given 15 minute period. Explanations for the resulting patterns of most popular shops can then be sought.
AT4/2b	9	Questionnaires involving people using local shops can concentrate on the identification of key features such as:

  (a) Which shops people visit regularly.

  (b) Which goods cannot be obtained locally.

  (c) The most popular larger local shopping centre.

  (d) The distance people have travelled to the local centre (from street names).

  (e) The method of travel used to visit the local shops.

  (f) The frequency of visits to the local shops.

  (g) How the centre could be improved.

AT1/3b	10	Children can devise a safety trail in the area immediately around the school. This would involve a series of points at which children could identify, map and explain an aspect of road safety important at that spot, e.g. a pedestrian crossing, a dangerous place to cross the road, a safe place to cross the road, problems from parked cars.

Although only geography ATs have been listed above, many of the activities provide opportunities for developing knowledge and skills in other subject areas, as well as cross-curricular elements (see 'Cross-curricular elements' on page 95).

A neighbourhood in Coventry

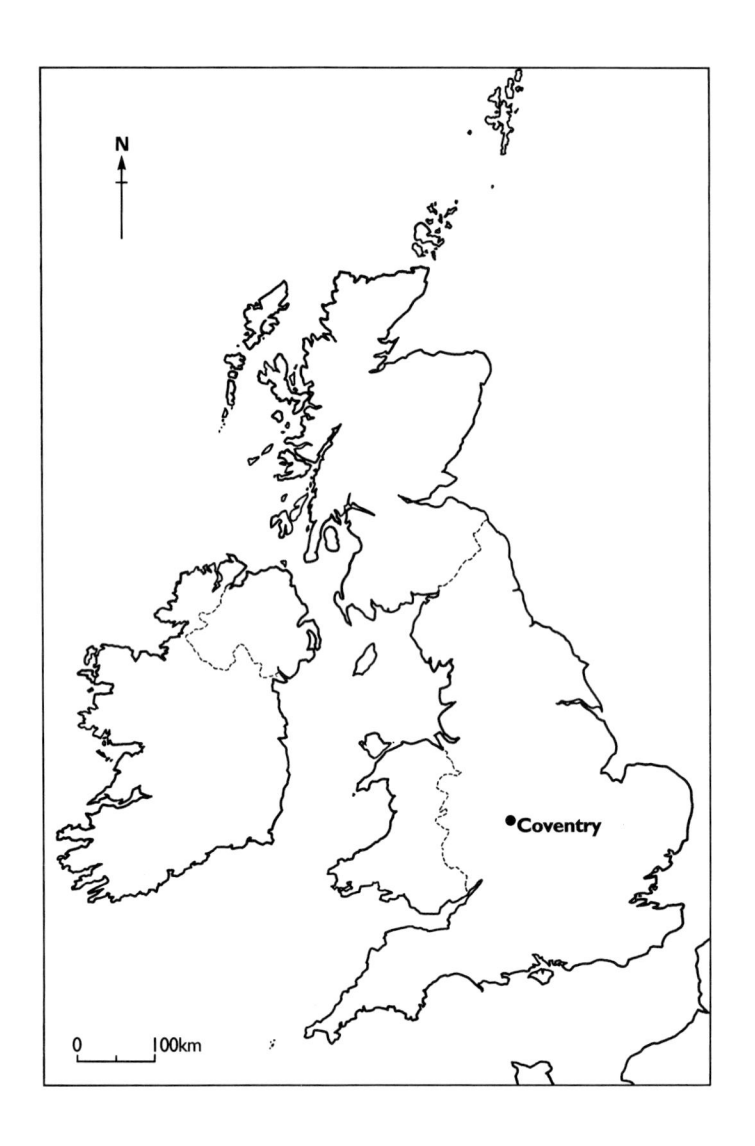

Related Copymasters 18-24	**Main Attainment Target**	AT2 Knowledge and Understanding of Places
	Key Statement of Attainment	*describe uses of land and buildings in the local area* (AT2/2b)
	Other relevant Statements of Attainment	AT1/2c, 2e, 3a, 3b, 3c, 3d AT2/2c, 2/3c, 3e, 3f AT4/2a, 2b, 2c, 3b, 3d AT5/2b

(Links between this unit, the Key Stage 1 Pupil Books and Book 2 are shown in the matrix on page 18 of this book.)

Using Oliver & Boyd Geography

1 Summary and purpose

The unit as a whole

The purpose of this unit is to examine the ways in which an urban neighbourhood in Coventry has changed, particularly within the last 100 years. The intention is to raise children's awareness of how much the present landscape is the result of changes from the past. It is important for children to understand the dynamic nature of their environment, whether that be urban or rural. All localities experience change, and this unit suggests some ways in which those changes can be investigated, through old maps, photographs and Trade Directories (most of which can usually be found in local libraries).

By showing the Edgwick area at different dates (through maps and photographs), the key idea of 'change over time' is made vivid, and also serves as a useful focus for local history studies, as well as providing a link to the history curriculum (especially units on the Victorians).

This unit can be used as the basis for a similar investigation by pupils in their own locality, or as the basis for comparisons between Coventry and their home locality and Coventry and Inverness. The unit revisits the Edgwick area of Coventry, first introduced in *Going to School* and *Living in a City,* at Key Stage 1. This time the focus is upon change through time within an urban locality.

Sub-units

Home and school introduces the two central characters, Jagdeep and Sukhdeep, and emphasises that schools, like neighbourhoods, often have both old and new parts. The picture map illustrates the layout of key elements of the urban area, such as the park and main roads in the zone near the school. It also makes links with the Inverness unit by reference to the identification of different house types in this Coventry locality.

Changes in the Blackwell Road area begins the process of helping children to identify clues as to how an area has changed. The land-use map on page 19 is important in establishing the type and location of houses in the part of Edgwick where Jagdeep and Sukhdeep live, as well as other buildings such as the pub, shops and factories. Then evidence from old photographs, and old maps (for 1890, 1910, 1930 and 1940) highlight in simple ways how the land use around the Blackwell Road area has changed.

Each of the maps on page 21 can be compared with the map on page 19 to demonstrate the nature, scale and location of the major changes.

Changes near Edgewick School shows how the area on the other side of the Foleshill Road, around the school, has changed since 1890. The three simple land use maps show exactly how the area has been built up, and the nature of each subsequent development, such as the expansion of the factory between 1910 and 1930. The maps also show the location of the different house types.

The photographs on page 24 provide an insight into past conditions in the factory (Edgwick Works) as well as an oblique aerial view of the surrounding area. It is important to make positive links between the maps (pages 19, 21, 23) and the aerial photograph on page 24. Children should be encouraged to identify and locate features on both maps and photographs. The last part of this section shows how the factory site has been redeveloped into an industrial estate.

Changes in Foleshill Road uses old photographs and information from Trade Directories to highlight changes in buildings, methods of transport and shops along the Foleshill Road. Similar work could be carried out by pupils in urban areas throughout the UK. The unit again emphasises the ways in which streets within urban areas change and develop over time. In particular, the conversion of houses to shops (linking with the Inverness unit) is strongly featured.

2 Background information

The multi-ethnic dimension is important in Edgwick, where a range of communities live close together, including people with close Irish links, people with close Polish or Hungarian links and people with close West Indian and particularly Asian links. It is important to remind children that the population of part of a town or city is constantly changing, as some people move in and others move away. The ethnic groups give diversity to this case study, and each group produces distinctive features of the urban environment such as places of worship or particular shop types. Children should be made aware of the elements common to all groups, such as the need for safety, food, clothing, heat, shelter, services and social contacts, as well as those elements specific to different groups.

Edgwick is one of Coventry's northern suburbs which has been developed over the last 100 years. It has many features typical of other UK urban areas, such as:

- a range of different house types (terraced, detached, etc.)
- a range of services such as shops, pubs, etc.
- buildings whose use has been changed
- both old and new buildings
- roads with dense traffic
- a pattern of land use which has changed several times over 100 years
- a pattern of land use which is closely related to past changes.

Many children live in areas with features similar to those in Edgwick, which can be investigated in similar ways using old maps, photographs and Directories.

(Note: The spelling of Edgwick when referring to the area is different from that of Edgewick Community Primary School.)

3 Key ideas

1. Schools often have both old and new sections.
2. There are different types of house in most areas.
3. Local areas change a lot in 100 years.
4. Edgwick School is very old.
5. Much of the area around Edgwick School has been built on for houses and factories.
6. Factories grow old and have to be replaced.
7. New factories and industrial estates develop.

8   Industrial estates contain many different workshops and factories.

9   Some parts of the Foleshill Road have changed little, others have changed a lot.

10 Methods of transport have changed over time.

11 Houses may be converted into shops.

12 Shops change – some close and new ones open.

4 Questions for discussion with the children

Home and school
Where – do Jagdeep and Sukhdeep live?
How – long does it take Jagdeep and Sukhdeep to get to school?
– do Jagdeep and Sukhdeep get to school?
Which – road do the children walk along to their school?

Changes in the Blackwell Road area
Where – were the houses built?
– were the shops built?
What – was the Blackwell Road area like in 1890?
– was the Blackwell Road area like in 1930?
– was the Blackwell Road area like in 1940?
– was on the site of Blackwell Road?
Which – buildings lasted from 1890 to 1940

Changes near Edgewick School
Where – is the industrial estate?
What – work went on in the factory on Canal Road?
– types of factories are on the industrial estate?
How – old is Edgewick School
Which – is the oldest primary school in Coventry?

Change in Foleshill Road
Where – did the trams run?
What – shops were there in Foleshill Road in 1991?
Why – is Foleshill Road dangerous for children?
How – have the shops changed?
When – did the trams stop running?

5 Links with Copymasters

Copymaster number and title	Main focus/purpose
18 The Blackwell Road area	Annotating large-scale plans
19 Making up symbols	Developing ideas on map symbols
20 People in the street	Classification of some jobs people do
21 Changes around Blackwell Road	Identification (on maps) of changes over time
22 An industrial estate	Classification of factories
23 Changes in Foleshill Road	Photo study to spot changes over time
24 Shops in Foleshill Road	Classification of shops

6 Further activities

AT4/2c

1. The children's own school can be a valuable starting point for activities which identify old and new parts of the building, together with investigations of old photographs, maps or school logs which may be available for some schools. Comparisons between past and present schools in terms of lessons, uniforms, classroom furniture and layout, discipline, teachers, types of work, games, meals and leisure can all contribute to the picture of change in and around the school. Children can write descriptions of a school day, both now and as it was 100 years ago. They can also describe the appearance of the school and its surrounding area, both now and 100 years ago.

AT4/2c, AT1/1b

2. Visits by parents, relatives, friends and older people who attended the school in the past can give a realistic touch to descriptions of school life fifty, sixty or seventy years ago. Children can prepare questions, then record answers, either in school or on visits to the homes of former pupils.

AT1/3d

3. Children can search for old photographs of the area around the school. Such photographs may come from Reference Libraries or personal collections, but they can form the starting point for activities highlighting the main changes in the local area. Key questions to be addressed include:

   - Why have some buildings/places changed very little?
   - Why have some buildings/places changed a great deal?
   - Which areas have changed most?
   - What has been the nature of the changes?
   - Why were the changes made?
   - How have the shops changed over time? Why?
   - Has the road layout changed? If so in what ways?

AT4/2a

4 Similarly, old maps, particularly the 1:2,500 and 1:5,000 produced by the Ordnance Survey, can be a vital element in any investigation of the local area. For example, names on the older maps may be preserved on modern versions as street names. It is important to use large scale maps which show as much detail as possible. However, the focus of study in the first instance should be a relatively small area, to enable pupils to become familiar with the maps and the features they show. In this way pupils can rapidly build up a detailed, accurate geography of their local area at different points in the past, e.g. in the 1970s, or the 1930s.

AT4/3d

5 Children can investigate the changing nature of local factory sites – some of which may survive intact, others may have disappeared from the map. This can be an introduction to the nature of factories, the type of activities they contain, and the ways in which they are responding to change. Comparisons between an old and a new factory are particularly useful, especially in relation to the reasons for their location at a particular site.

AT4/2c, AT1/3b

6 Local Trade Directories can be used to identify land uses in the area around the school. If a series of dates is taken, such as 1900, 1930, 1950, 1970 and the present, the pattern of change in the shops along a street, or the factories along a canal, can be identified, mapped, described and analysed.

AT1/3d

7 Oblique aerial photographs of the school and its surroundings at different dates can be analysed, to identify different and changing land uses. Later, vertical air photographs can be compared with large scale maps of the locality and features can be identified on both.

AT2/3f

8 Children can select features of the locality such as shops (or one type of shop, e.g. a newsagent or baker), factories or services such as the post office, or bus station or railway station, and attempt to explain their location. The important question is, 'Why is it here?' In order to answer this, other key questions are:

- Is transport important? e.g. By road, rail, air, water, or on foot.
- Where do the raw materials, e.g. newspapers, come from? How do they get here?
- Where do the products go? Do people call in? Are the products transported? If so, what types of transport are used?
- Where does the workforce come from? Do the workers live locally? Do they have to travel? If so, how do they travel?
- Is this a point where routes meet? If so, which routes and where from?

Although only geography ATs have been listed above, many of the activities provide opportunities for developing knowledge and skills in other subject areas, as well as cross-curricular elements (see 'Cross-curricular elements' on page 95).

Quarries and Mines

3 Slate from North Wales
   Slate and its uses
   The old slate mines
   Slate quarrying today
   Tourists come to Llechwedd
   Slate all around

4 Coal mining in Yorkshire
   Coal and its uses
   Open-cast mining
   Coal under Yorkshire
   The work of the miners
   From coal to electricity
   Changes in mining

Using Oliver & Boyd Geography

Slate from North Wales

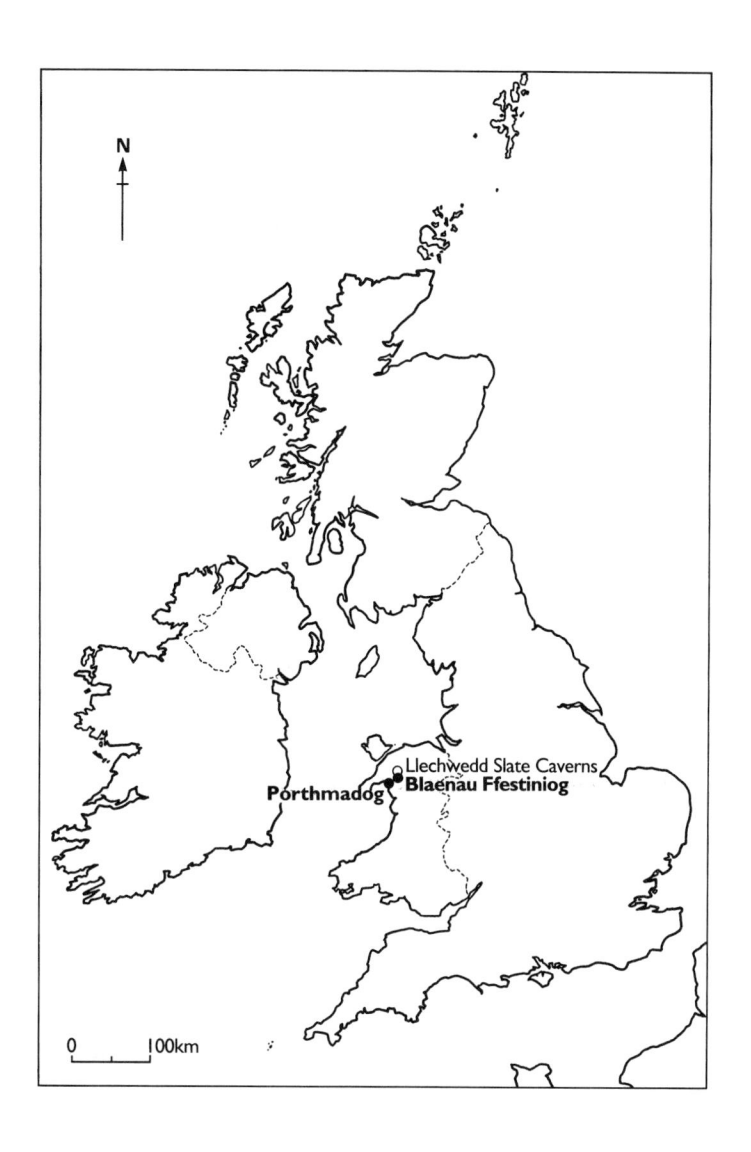

Related Copymasters 25-32		
	Main Attainment Target	AT5 Environmental Geography
	Key Statements of Attainment	*identify how people obtain materials from the environment* (AT5/2a)
		describe effects on environments of extracting natural resources (AT5/3a)
	Other relevant Statements of Attainment	AT1/2a, 2e, 3a, 3d AT2/3c, 3e, 3f AT4/3b, 3c, 3d AT5/2b

(Links between this unit, the Key Stage 1 Pupil Books and Book 2 are shown in the matrix on page 18 of this book.)

1 Summary and purpose

The unit as a whole

The purpose of this unit is to examine the process by which materials are obtained from natural resources (AT5). Slate is a good example of such a natural resource, being a rock occurring naturally in the landscape which has become very useful both throughout the UK and other parts of the world, where there are thousands of homes with slate roofs.

The unit explains why people have found slate so useful, both now and in the past, and how the slate is extracted from the ground by quarrying or mining (past and present). An important aspect of the unit is the effect that mining and quarrying have in changing the environment.

The intention is to provide a specific example of a commonly occurring natural resource with which most children will be familiar. Through a study of slate, children will be able to consider what makes slate such a good natural resource; where and how it can be obtained; and how it has affected the areas from which it is quarried or mined.

Sub-units

Slate and its uses identifies some of the main uses for the rock – for housing, for writing materials in some parts of the world, and even for gravestones. Notice the short but concise definitions of quarrying (on the surface) and mining (underground extraction). The location of the important slate mining areas around Blaenau Ffestiniog is then highlighted, together with the idea of people moving into the area and building houses and settlements as work became available.

The old slate mines considers how slate was extracted in the past. It also makes a point that is worth emphasising, namely that slate is found both on the surface and underground – children sometimes have difficulty in understanding that some resources have to be extracted from underground. Details of past mining techniques and their limitations are considered, particularly in relation to quarrying and splitting the rock. Mining and quarrying such a heavy resource soon led to the construction of the Ffestiniog Railway, connecting the mines with Porthmadog on the coast. The present use of the railway as a tourist attraction highlights the ways in which past industrial activities can be exploited in relation to the modern tourist industry

Slate quarrying today uses the Llechwedd quarries to show how conditions have changed. The use of modern machines and technology has streamlined the process, requiring fewer people to produce all the slate needed. Nevertheless, some processes-notably slate splitting- are still done by hand and so depend on human skills. The use of lorries instead of rail transport is another important change in quarry activity.

Tourists come to Llechwedd The decline in the demand for slate, as other materials such as artificial tiles have been used to replace it, leads to this section. The decline of slate mining and quarrying has encouraged local people to seek alternative uses for the mines and quarries, and for the employment of ex-miners. Tourism is one such alternative, providing visitors with a chance to go underground and experience conditions under which the slate miners laboured. It is important to note that some of the guides are men who used to work in the mines before they were closed.

Slate all around summarises through maps and photographs the impact that mining and quarrying have had on the local environment. In particular, it emphasises the waste tips and the huge holes in the ground left when quarrying ends.

2 Background information

A resource is something that people find useful. In the distant past, slate was simply another rock in the landscape. However, when people began to realise that it had uses, it became a resource. The main uses were developed in the nineteenth century, when its value as a roofing material was recognised. The rapid growth of Victorian towns, with their row upon row of terraced houses, created a huge demand for a roofing material which was abundant, strong, cheap, easy to work and weatherproof. Slate met all these criteria. Whilst not universally available, there are large deposits in places such as North Wales, where these older rocks are to be found at or near the surface. Railways were built to move the heavy, bulky slate from mines and quarries to ports from which ships carried it off to other parts of the UK and the world. The Ffestiniog Railway opened in 1836 and was abandoned in 1946. The first passenger section was re-opened in 1955.

Slate is a *metamorphic* rock, that is one which has been changed in the distant past by heat and pressure. In the geological past, movements in the earth's crust generated this heat and pressure, which in turn gave slate its unique characteristics as a hard rock which cleaves (splits) easily into thin sheets. It was this facility to split the rock which made slate cheap and attractive to house builders. It is also strong and weatherproof.

The early extraction was in quarries where the slate outcropped on the surface. It was hard, demanding work and wages were not high. However, the prospect of an alternative to farming encouraged many people to migrate to places like Blaenau and set up home. New houses, shops, pubs, schools and chapels were built, using the locally quarried slate.

Soon, much of the slate on the surface had been extracted, so mines had to be sunk to tap underground deposits. Early mining technology was effective but crude and time consuming.

In order to extract the slate, other rock had to be mined and removed. This was waste as far as the miners were concerned, and so was dumped in heaps close to both the mines and the houses of the workers. These spoil heaps grew rapidly and came to dominate the skyline. Initially this was not a problem because the surrounding land was of little agricultural value. During the nineteenth century, places such as Blaenau were growth points in the UK economy. Railways brought more people and prosperity. Communities grew, expanded and developed. The population of Ffestiniog Parish was 4553 in 1861, and 11 433 in 1901, the year when it reached its maximum.

The decline of slate mining and quarrying began in the 1920s when tiles became available as a cheaper, more readily available roofing material. Slate mining was also affected by the wars, when many miners were called up, and by slumps and booms of housebuilding within the rest of Britain. In addition, there were problems about using modern quarrying machinery in the old mines because of narrow passageways and the dangers of fuel fumes. As the demand for slate declined, people lost their jobs. With no other local sources of employment people moved away and communities began to change and decay, whilst quarries and mines closed. At Llechwedd there is still an active quarry and slate mill, but output is very small compared with that in the past.

As more people left the area, services such as shops, pubs and even chapels closed. Recently, the growth of tourism has provided a lifeline for some of the quarries and mines, though relatively few people are employed in them. Meanwhile, around the towns and villages of North Wales the scars of mining and quarrying remain – huge holes gouged out of the earth and

The output of slate from Llechwedd Slate mines

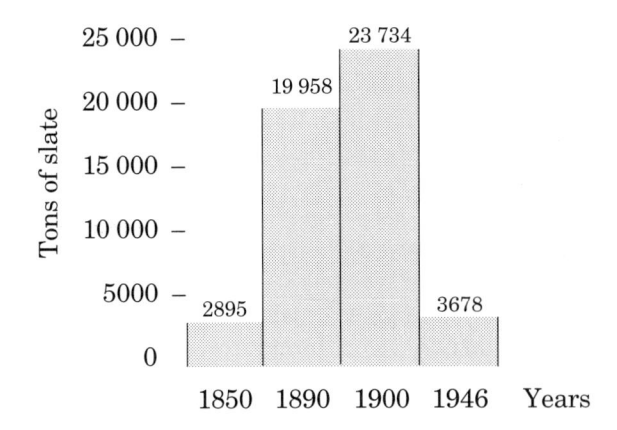

Year	Tons of slate
1850	2895
1890	19 958
1900	23 734
1946	3678

unsightly tip heaps towering above rows of houses. Some quarries have been partially filled, but many more remain. The cost of reclamation more than anything delays further improvements, and there are few economical uses for the slate debris.

Attempts have been made to flatten some of the tips in parts of North Wales, and tips have been planted with trees and grass to make areas of parkland. In Blaenau, where many ex-slate workers still live, there is strong local pride and even affection for the tips.

3 Key ideas

1. Slate is a metamorphic rock.
2. Slate has many uses.
3. Slate can be split, cut and carved.
4. Most slate in Britain comes from North Wales.
5. Slate can be quarried on the surface or mined underground.
6. Towns grew up when slate was mined.
7. Slate is found in veins underground.
8. Mining in the past was slow, unhealthy work. Many miners died from lung diseases caused by slate dust.
9. Explosives were used to break up the rock.
10. The slate was sawn and split in special mills.
11. Hammers and chisels were and are used to split the slate into thin roofing slates.
12. Steam trains transported the slate to the coast.
13. Today, quarrying is more mechanised, and large machines dig down to the slate pillars left in the old mines to hold up the cavern roofs.
14. Quarries are often very deep.
15. Today, lorries transport the slate.
16. The old slate mines have become tourist attractions.
17. Waste tips from mining and quarrying surround towns such as Blaenau.

4 Questions for discussion with the children

Slate and its uses
Where – does most slate in Britain come from?
What – is slate used for? – is mining? – is quarrying?
Why – did Blaenau grow?
When – was Blaenau Ffestiniog built?

The old slate mines
Where – is slate found?
– were the slate blocks sawn up and split?
– did the railway start?
What – are veins?
– was gunpowder used for?
– were jumpers?
How – did miners reach the slate?
– long did it take to dig one metre in the past?
– was the slate taken to the surface?
– was the slate split?
When – was the Ffestiniog Railway built?

Slate quarrying today
Where – are the Llechwedd quarries?
What – are used to dig the slate?
Why – are quarries so deep?
When – did quarrying start at Llechwedd?
How – are the blocks cut into smaller pieces?
– are the slates transported?

Tourists come to Llechwedd
Where – do tourists visit at Llechwedd?
– did some guides work before they became guides?
How – do the shops look?
Who – show visitors round?

Slate all round
Where – will people see slate near Blaenau Ffestiniog?
What – are waste tips?
– are the tips like?
Why – were waste tips needed?
When – were the tips made?

5 Links with Copymasters

Copymaster number and title	Main focus/purpose
25 Around Blaenau Ffestiniog	Mapwork/use of atlas
26 Living near a quarry	Analysis of problems caused by quarrying and possible solutions
27 Llechwedd slate caverns	Route-finding exercise on a plan
28 A gravel pit	Environmental impact of gravel extraction and repairing damaged environments
29 A slate town in North Wales	Mapwork, identifying key places
30 The Ffestiniog railway	Pictorial mapwork
31 Moving around	Different types of transport and their advantages/disadvantages for moving different goods
32 Blaenau from above	Analysis of an air photograph

6 Further activities

AT5/2a

1. Children can make collections of natural resources such as wood, coal, granite, slate, limestone, chalk, together with wool, fish, cotton, vegetable oil, wheat and potatoes. They can then investigate the origin of each resource and the methods used to extract or produce it.

AT5/2a

2. Groups of children can research the environmental effects of extracting a particular resource, for example, methods used to catch different types of fish (*pelagic* and *demersal*) and the dangers of overfishing. Similarly, another group could investigate the forestry industry, and produce a flow diagram of timber from tree to pulp mill, together with the environmental effects of planting large areas of the uplands with coniferous forests.

AT5/2b

3. The use of slate in the area around the school could lead to a further investigation of other rocks used in local buildings. Examples of marble, sandstone, chalk, flint, granite and basalt, are widely used.

AT3/1a

4. Collections of different types of rock are an important part of geography at all stages. Children should be encouraged to make their own collections of as many different types as they can find, and to bring to school objects from home which are made from slate and other natural materials. Group activities involving sorting rocks into sets on criteria determined by the children in terms of, for example, colour, shape, texture, or size, may be the start of further work on the properties of the different rock types. Simple group experiments can determine characteristics such as *hardness* (test with the fingernail, and a piece of steel), *weight, density, appearance* (including colour), *surface texture* (e.g. smooth, crumbly, rounded, sharp-edged) and *reaction to water* (dripped on to the surface). Such work can also link with science work on materials.

AT4/3c

5　Pupils can investigate the suitability of different types of transport for different goods. For example, water or rail transport was ideal for slate, because it is such a heavy, bulky material. The relative merits of different types of transport (canal, ship, lorry, car, aeroplane, train) in terms of speed, cost, and capacity can be related to the shipment of specific items, e.g. diamonds from Brazil to London, fresh cut flowers from France to Birmingham, steel from Germany to Southampton, cars from France to Hull, or letters from Hong Kong to Inverness.

AT5/3a

6　The relative costs and benefits of extracting a natural resource such as slate can be discussed with the children. The intention is to demonstrate that people may hold conflicting views about the costs and benefits of resource extraction. For example, local unemployed people may resent the run down of slate mining, whilst outsiders may see the decline of slate mining as a good opportunity to improve the waste tips, mines and abandoned quarries. Role play can be useful in this context, with groups given role cards such as:

- local unemployed people (dislike the run down of mining)
- tourists visiting Llechwedd (dislike waste tips but like to visit the mines)
- local farmers (resent the loss of land)
- local shopkeepers (fewer local people shopping but some tourist trade)
- local estate agents (empty houses and few takers)
- local households (dislike being objects of curiosity for the tourists)
- old miners (like jobs as tourist guides)

7　Pupils who live within easy reach of the North Wales area could be taken to visit some of the old slate mines and the slate museums. Booklets are also available from some of them (e.g. Quarry Tours Ltd., Llechwedd Slate Caverns, Blaenau Ffestiniog, Gwynedd LL41 3NB. (Telephone 0766 830306.)

Although only geography ATs have been listed above, many of the activities provide opportunities for developing knowledge and skills in other subject areas, as well as cross-curricular elements (see 'Cross-curricular elements' on page 95).

Coal mining in Yorkshire

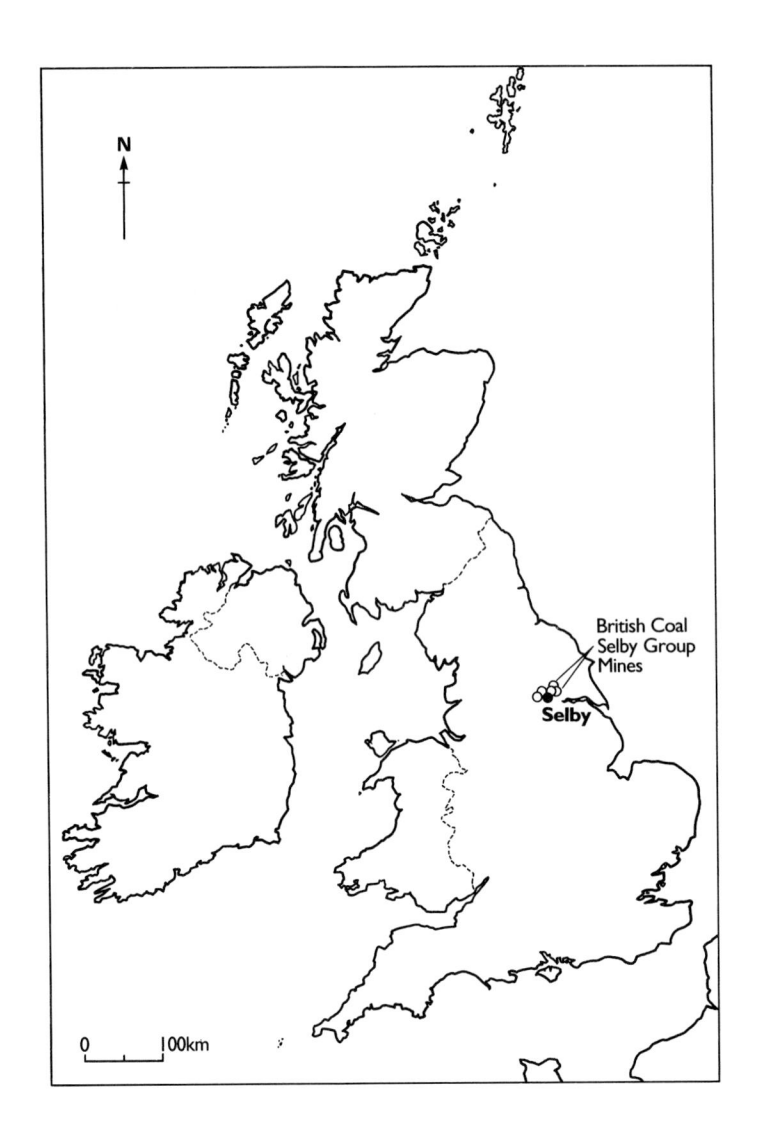

Related Copymasters 33-42	**Main Attainment Target**	AT5 Environmental Geography
	Key Statements of Attainment	*identify how people obtain materials from the environment* (AT5/2a)
		describe effects on environments of extracting natural resources (AT5/3a)
	Other relevant Statements of Attainment	AT1/2a, 2e, 3a, 3d AT2/3c, 3e, 3f AT4/3c, 3d AT5/2b

(Links between this unit, the Key Stage 1 Pupil Books and Book 2 are shown in the matrix on page 18 of this book.)

Using Oliver & Boyd Geography

1 Summary and purpose

The unit as a whole

The purpose of this unit is to inform children of the nature, location and importance of a major natural UK resource, namely coal. The unit specifically links coal to electricity generation because it is in this form that most children will encounter the power source, and because electricity generation is the most important market for British coal. Coal and power are two themes fundamental to an understanding of British industrial, urban and environmental geography.

It is important for children to be aware of the country's main energy sources, and of the importance of power and energy in people's everyday lives. Virtually all homes and schools are lit by electricity and have multifarious electric gadgets. Most aspects of everyday life from making a hot drink to playing a computer game depend on energy. It is also important for children to be aware of the environmental effects that result from mining coal.

Sub-units

Coal and its uses describes how homes used to be heated by coal, but that now most coal is turned into electricity, though significant amounts do go to other uses such as steel making.

Opencast mining identifies the location of coal seams in the ground with some seams close to the surface. In these cases opencast mining can take place. The mechanised nature of opencast mining, its effects on the countryside and the need to replace the soil, plants and trees after mining are further important points.

Coal under Yorkshire is a case study of the Selby coalfield. This is a deep coalfield which has some of the most modern mines in the country, with large, mechanised pits using the latest mining techniques.

The work of the miners describes the different jobs in the Selby coalfield, necessary to get the coal from the face to the power station. This section also describes some of the problems of underground mining, such as the darkness, the heat and the dust.

From coal to electricity describes the pattern of Selby mines and the railway link between Gascoigne Wood Mine (where the coal is sorted) and Drax Power Station (to which all the coal from the new Selby mines is sent).

Changes in mining contrasts mining conditions 100 years ago, and the settlements which grew up around them, with the modern mines described in the earlier parts of the unit. It also points out how some miners have moved home from old to new mining areas, whilst others commute from their original homes near the older mines to the new ones.

2 Background information

Coal mining is an important UK industry which is currently experiencing rapid change. Coal was the power behind the nineteenth century Industrial Revolution. Throughout the century coal was a growth industry with large exports to the rest of the world. The coalfields in South Wales, Scotland, Yorkshire, Lancashire, the Midlands and the North East became centres of industry and of towns. Coal mining areas were characterised by rows of terraced houses close to spoil heaps and the pithead winding gear. Whole communities grew up dependent on the pit.

Conditions changed after the 1950s when alternatives to coal such as oil and gas became more available. The markets for coal began to decline both at home and abroad. In many coalfields, the thickest seams closest to the surface had been worked out. Coal still remains, but it is in deeper, more faulted (broken) seams and so more expensive to mine. British Coal has therefore been closing pits on the older coalfields. This has led to the loss of many jobs, and to serious social problems for those communities, now in decline, which grew up around the pit. At the same time, British Coal has invested in new, deeper mines on the new coalfields of Selby in Yorkshire and the Vale of Belvoir in Leicestershire. In these areas new jobs have been created (though mechanisation is high so the numbers are not large) and some miners have moved into the new areas.

The changing fortunes of the British coal industry can be seen in the following figures:

1 Number of miners (UK)

1920	1 000 000
1940	800 000
1960	450 000
1980	200 000
1990	56 000

2 UK coal production

1920	260 million tonnes
1940	210 million tonnes
1960	175 million tonnes
1980	100 million tonnes
1990	75 million tonnes

3 Output per miner (in tonnes per year)

1940	212
1960	310
1980	476
1990	499

4 Percentage of UK coal cut by machine

1960	7
1970	38
1980	94
1990	97

British Coal is trying to reduce costs by using more opencast mining sites. This is a much cheaper method of coal extraction, but it can be much more harmful for the environment. Local residents object to proposals for opencast sites in their area because of the increase in lorry traffic, noise, dust and pollution which accompany such ventures. British Coal point to their record of restoring opencast sites to their original condition (or better) by replacing the soil and vegetation cover.

The future of British coalmining is currently unclear for a variety of reasons:

1. The Electricity Companies are the most important market for coal. However, the companies are keen to buy the cheapest coal, which in some cases is that which is imported from countries such as the USA, China and South Africa. British Coal is therefore trying to reduce the costs of mining operations wherever possible.

2. British coal burned in power stations generates acid rain. This is because most British coal contains a high concentration of sulphur dioxide. Imported coal contains less sulphur dioxide and it would be cheaper to buy it in order to reduce sulphur dioxide emissions from the power stations.

3 British Coal may be privatised at some point in the future.

4 The environmental impact of coal mining has received much attention in the UK.

Hence the British coal industry is entering a period of rapid and dramatic change. This is another reason for its inclusion in any study of modern UK geography.

3 Key ideas

1 Coal is a natural resource.
2 Coal used to be the main source of heat.
3 Coal is burned to generate electricity.
4 Coal is found in seams in the ground.
5 Coal seams close to the surface are mined by opencast methods.
6 Opencast mining is very mechanised.
7 Opencast mining damages the countryside.
8 After mining the soil, trees and plants are replaced.
9 Coal is mined in tunnels underground.
10 Much mining is done by machines.
11 Mine shafts link the surface with the underground coal seams, and lift cages carry the miners up and down.
12 Underground trains take miners to the coal face.
13 Working underground is hot and noisy, and some of it is done without lighting.
14 Miners wear lamps on their helmets to help them to see underground.
15 Machines cut the coal.
16 Conveyor belts bring the coal to the surface.
17 Rocks and dirt are removed from the coal.
18 Coal goes by rail to the power station.
19 Power lines carry electricity to centres of demand.
20 Old coal mines employed more men and fewer machines.
21 Villages and towns grew up around old coal mines.
22 Many old coal mines have closed.
23 Some miners have moved to new mines.
24 New houses have been built near the new mines.

4 Questions for discussion with the children

Coal and its uses

Where – is electricity made/produced?

– is coal found?

What – was coal used for in the past?

– are the other modern uses of coal?

– are coal seams?

– is opencast mining?

– happens when opencast mining ends?

Coal under Yorkshire

Where – is Selby?

– is the coal?

– is the coal sorted?

What – is the land like near Selby?

– do much of the work?

– does the control room do?

– are used to cut the coal?

– carry electricity from power stations to homes?

How – many coal mines are there at Selby?

– does the coal reach Gascoigne Wood?

– are miners carried down to the coal seam?

– do the miners reach the coal face?

– does the coal reach Drax Power Station?

Which – work is hot and noisy?

Why – do miners wear lamps on their helmets?

Changes in mining

Where – are some of the modern coal mines?

– did old villages and towns grow up?

What – has happened to miners from the old pits?

– has been built near the new mines?

– are the differences between the old and the new miners' homes?

How – do most miners get to work?

– do old and new mines differ at the surface?

Why – are there large car parks next to modern mines?

Using Oliver & Boyd Geography

5 Links with Copymasters

Copymaster number and title	Main focus/purpose
33 Opencast coal mining	Defines key elements of opencast mining and the environment
34 Britain's coalfields	Names and locates main coalfields through atlas work
35 An old coal mine	Describes surface and underground features of an old underground mine
36 A miner's day in 1920	Plotting activities at different times of day on pie graph
37 A miner's day in 1990	As above
38 An opencast coal mine	Analysis of an air photograph
39 Coal mining today	Recognition of different activities in a modern mine
40 The Selby Coalfield	Mapwork based on the eight points of the compass
41 Coal mining in the Selby area	Sequencing activity using sketches of stages from coal extraction to electricity generation
42 Changes in a mining area	Examines the changes to a coal mining area over time

6 Further activities

AT5/1a, 2a

1   Groups of children can be given samples of coal, and test them for:
- appearance and colour;
- hardness (test with fingernail and a piece of steel);
- weight;
- surface texture;
- reaction to water (dripped onto the surface);
- fossils e.g. prints of ferns, or other plants or animals.

AT5/2a, 3a

2   Research activities should help pupils to describe and explain the formation of coal, from living trees which fell and were covered by the sea and other rocks, to the effects of heat and pressure over millions of years, changing the wood into coal. Booklets produced by British Coal are useful for individual or group research. (British Coal Public Relations, Hobart House, Grosvenor Place, London SW1X 7AE, and British Coal Opencast, 200, Lichfield Lane, Berry Hill, Mansfield, Notts NG18 4RG.)

AT5/3a 3 Other topics suitable for individual or group investigation using materials from British Coal are:

- different methods of mining coal, e.g. Bell Pits, Board and Pillar, and Longwall;
- coal's importance in the Industrial Revolution;
- inventors linked with coal, e.g. George Stephenson, James Watt, Sir Humphry Davy;
- modern uses of coal;
- smokeless fuels;
- transporting coal;
- exploring for new coalfields;
- restoring land after opencast mining.

AT5/3b 4 Photographs and maps from British Coal Opencast can be used to compare an area before and after opencast mining and the restoration of the area. Pupils can identify key points in pictures and maps and describe the nature of the changes each has undergone. It is also useful to collect press reports of public protests to proposed new opencast sites.

AT5/2a 5 Children can draw a series of pictures to show the formation and development of coal. Such pictures can then be sequenced with appropriate written commentaries as part of an overall display on coal.

AT4/3b 6 The pie diagrams of a miner's day in the 1920s and in the 1990s can form the basis of creative writing. Pupils can imagine they are a 1990s miner and can record on tape the sequence of events in a typical day. Contrasts between the 1920s and the 1990s can then be highlighted, together with questions requiring further research, e.g. What type of house did 1920s miners live in? What were they like?

AT4/3d 7 Children can design and make a simple 3-dimensional cross-section of a coal mine to show the surface buildings and winding gear, the shafts, the coal seams, tunnels and other details. Arrows can be located to illustrate the movement of coal from seam to surface.

AT5/4c 8 In order to consider some of the environmental effects of opencast mining, pupils could consider how they would feel if an opencast pit were developed close to where they live. What would be the main problems (lorry traffic, noise, dust, pollution, loss of countryside) and what would be the main benefits (jobs, customers for some shops)?

AT1/4c 9 Ordnance Survey maps of older coal mining areas, such as South Wales, North East England, Central Scotland or West Yorkshire, can be used to identify the key features of such areas, e.g. abandoned railway lines, abandoned mines, spoil heaps and tips, and rows of terraced houses. These maps can then be supplemented by air photographs of older mining areas and features from the maps can be identified and labelled on the photographs. Maps and photographs of the newer coalfields can be compared for similarities and differences.

Although only geography ATs have been listed above, many of the activities provide opportunities for developing knowledge and skills in other subject areas, as well as cross-curricular elements (see 'Cross-curricular elements' on page 95).

People on the Move

5 Moving to the coast: Southport
   Welcome to Southport!
   Homes for old people in Southport
   Southport in the past
   Moving around in Southport

6 On the move in the Sahel
   A Village in Burkina Faso
   Finding food
   The magic stones
   The firewood and water trail
   Finding work

Moving to the coast : Southport

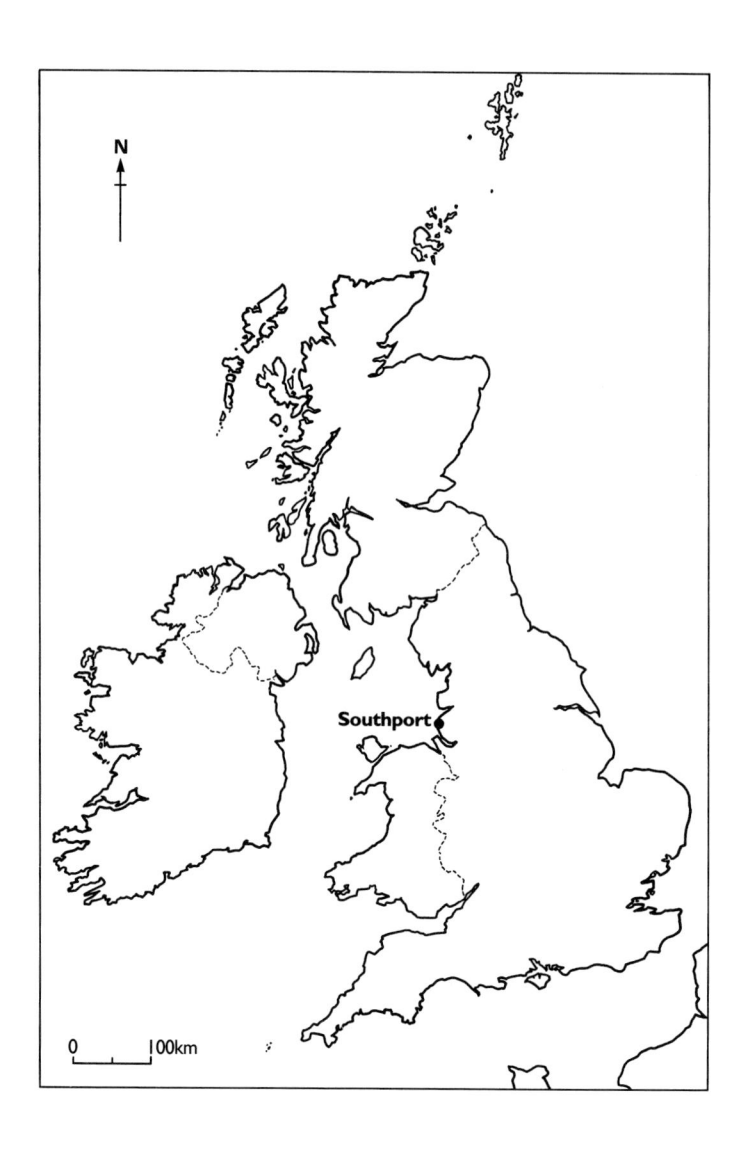

Related Copymasters 43-47	**Main Attainment Target**	AT4 Human Geography
	Key Statements of Attainment	*give reasons why people make journeys of different lengths* (AT4/2b)
		give reasons why people change their homes (AT4/3a)
	Other relevant Statements of Attainment	AT1/2a, 2e, 3a, 3d AT2/3e, 3f AT4/2c, 3b, 3c, 3d

(Links between this unit, the Key Stage 1 Pupil Books and Book 2 are shown in the matrix on page 18 of this book.)

Using Oliver & Boyd Geography

1 Summary and purpose

The unit as a whole

This unit is designed to develop one of the reasons why people move homes (AT 4/3a), namely when they retire to the coast. Other reasons for people moving home covered in this book include: changing jobs (see *Coal mining in Yorkshire*); and searching for new jobs and services (see *On the move in the Sahel*).

The unit also uses maps and photographs to highlight the key features of a particular type of settlement (AT4/3b) namely a seaside resort. Other themes covered in this unit include: the effects of population change on settlements e.g. more retirement homes in Southport; and the ways in which UK resorts have changed over the last 70 years.

Sub-units

Welcome to Southport! introduces the meaning of retirement and uses two fictional characters, Mr and Mrs Jennings, as a way in to studying Southport as a retirement town. The facilities available to both retired residents and visitors in the seaside resort are then described through pictures.

Homes for old people in Southport focuses on the ways in which the urban environment of the town reflects its changing population. The growing importance of flats, rest homes and nursing homes in Southport is described, as are the differences between them.

Southport in the past uses old photographs and maps to show how the elements of the resort have changed. It also explains how and why people from the crowded industrial towns of Lancashire visited places such as Southport on their days out. The pureness of coastal air in contrast to the pollution in places such as Preston is emphasised, together with the importance of cheap rail travel in enabling people from all walks of life to visit Southport. Other attractions of the resort, such as the pier, promenade, lakes and swimming pools, are also described.

Moving around in Southport uses photographs to make direct comparisons between methods of transport now and in the past. Contrasts in public forms of transport such as trams and buses, and personal forms of transport such as wheel chairs, are also highlighted.

2 Background information

For most people proximity to their place of work determines where they live. However, once they retire this need no longer apply. More and more people in Britain are choosing to move home after they retire, and coastal areas are the most popular destinations.

At present about 10 per cent of people move when they reach retirement, and the figure is still increasing.

Not all people can afford to move when they retire, so this type of migration is selective. It is largely the better-off people from higher socio-economic groups with a home to sell, who are the ones who can afford to move.

The proportion of Britain's population aged 65 and over is rising steadily and will continue to do so for the foreseeable future. In 1969, only 15.9 per cent of the UK population was above retirement age (60 for females, 65 for males) but by 1979 this had risen to 17.3 per cent and by 1989 to 18.2 per cent.

There is also a growing tendency for more people to retire early, which will further swell the numbers. Similarly, the percentage of people owning their own home has increased from 49 per cent in 1969 to 67 per cent in 1989. So more people will have homes to sell and be able to buy flats or houses in towns such as Southport.

The most attractive areas for retired people are those with a pleasant, semi-rural environment, a mild climate and on the coast. Hence Cornwall and Devon are particularly popular, together with the south and east coast of England, parts of Wales, north west and north east England. Familiarity with resorts, because of day trips or holidays, is often a reason for people choosing their place of retirement, as is proximity to relatives who may still live in the places from which people move. There is a strong link between areas of high urban population, and clusters of coastal resorts and retirement towns (e.g. London and the south coast, Yorkshire and Scarborough, etc.).

Holiday resorts such as Southport are not new. The Romans used Bath as a holiday resort. In the eighteenth century it became fashionable for richer members of society to 'take the waters' at spas like Brighton and Harrogate. Later, in the nineteenth century, the new railways allowed many more people to visit the coast. (See map on page 59.) Thousands of people flocked from big cities like Glasgow, Manchester and London, to coastal resorts. Weston-super-Mare, Southport, Clacton and Rhyl all grew at this time. Even in the 1950s, most people still had only one or two weeks paid holiday each year, and spent them at British coastal resorts such as Eastbourne and Scarborough. The impression of clean, unpolluted air and a relaxed, semi-rural environment persuaded many people in later life to retire to places like Southport. Not all retired people are inactive or infirm. They enjoy a wide range of leisure pursuits, ranging from golf and other sports to indoor entertainments.

3 Key ideas

1 When people retire they may move house.

2 Some retired people go to live in coastal resorts.

3 Settlements where many retired people live have facilities such as parks and flats.

4 In the past, people from the industrial towns of Lancashire made day trips to places like Southport.

5 Familiarity due to past day trips or holidays is a reason for choosing Southport as a retirement town.

6 The clean air, sunshine and sea breezes attracted visitors to places like Southport.

7 Industrial centres such as Preston were crowded and suffered from air pollution.

8 The railways enabled many people from the cities to make day trips to Southport.

9 Southport's attractions included the pier and the promenade.

10 Special apartments have been built for retired people.

11 Houses have been converted into rest homes.

12 Nursing homes have increased in number.

13 Methods of getting around have changed in the last 80 years.

4 Questions for discussion with the children

Welcome to Southport!

Where – do retired people move to?

– did Mr and Mrs Jennings move from?

What – happens when people retire?

When – did Mr and Mrs Jennings receive their card?

– do people retire?

– do some people move house?

Southport in the past

Where – are the pier and the promenade?

What – sort of town is Preston?

– did Mr and Mrs Jennings like about Southport?

Why – were seaside towns healthier than industrial cities?

When – did Mr and Mrs Jennings first visit Southport?

How – could people travel to Southport?

Homes for old people in Southport

What – is an apartment?

– is a rest home?

– is a nursing home?

Who – live in a rest home?

– looks after people in a nursing home?

Why – are there so many rest homes and nursing homes in Southport?

Moving around in Southport

What – is the main shopping street of Southport?

– are bath chairs?

Why – do some people need a wheelchair?

How – did people get around 80 years ago?

– do people travel around Southport now?

When – did few people own a car?

5 Links with Copymasters

Copymaster number and title	Main focus/purpose
43 Why move to Southport?	Examines 'push' and 'pull' factors in migration of retired people to coastal resorts
44 Southport's sea front	Mapwork using coordinates
45 Southport from above	Analysis of oblique air photographs
46 Using Southport's parks	Uses bar graphs to classify uses of parks
47 In the park	Mapwork to locate features in a park

6 Further activities

AT4/2b
1. A class survey can produce numbers of relatives over the retirement age. This can lead to work using a simple database to present the information in bar charts.

AT4/3b
2. Children can use a graphics package to produce leaflets and posters advertising the attractions of Southport, or a similar coastal centre for retired people. Their results can be compared with other groups who can make posters using traditional methods.

AT4/3b, AT1/3d
3. Air photographs and maps can be used to identify key features, such as the pier, swimming pools, main streets, the railways station, etc.

AT2/2c
4. On a visit to an old people's home, or alternatively during a school visit by senior citizens, the children can record the thoughts and impressions of the people involved. This can form the basis of imaginative descriptions of what life used to be like for local people.

AT4/3b
5. A class survey of UK coastal resorts visited can form the basis of mapwork identifying the most frequently visited centre. Is it the nearest? If not, why is it so attractive? Is it attractive to both old and young people?

AT4/3a
6. Children can design and make a selection of retirement cards, suitable for people in a range of occupations. The work would involve consideration of the images of the future which the card should contain, and how these might relate to present occupations.

AT4/3b
7. The class can visit the local reference library and/or study early photographs of coastal scenes in Victorian/Edwardian/1920s resorts. These can be compared with modern photographs to highlight similarities and differences.

AT1/4e
8. Map and atlas activities can arise from this unit, e.g. name the four industrial towns closest to Southport (or Clacton, Brighton, Ayr, etc.). Name the nearest motorway and main road. In which direction are Manchester, Preston, Liverpool, Leeds, etc. from Southport?

AT2/3f
9. Children can use commercial directories to map the location of nursing homes and retirement homes in their local area. Why do they seem to concentrate in certain streets or areas within the towns?

On the move in the Sahel

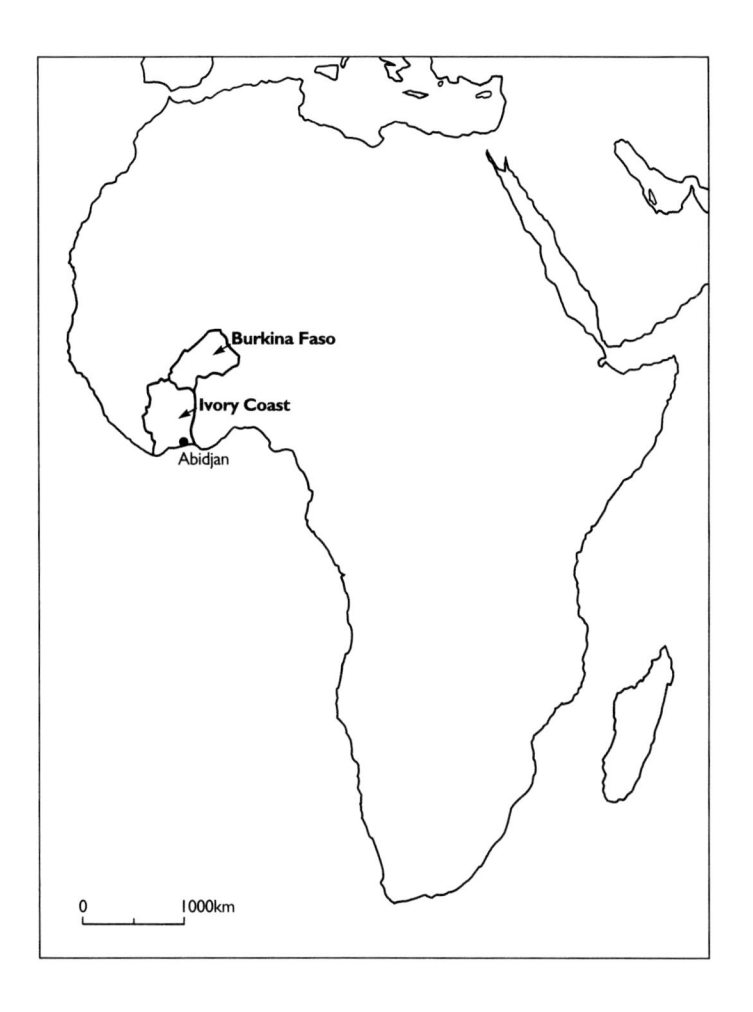

Related Copymasters		
48-54	**Main Attainment Target**	AT4 Human Geography
	Key Statements of Attainment	*give reasons why people make journeys of different lengths* (AT4/2b)
		give reasons why people change their homes (AT4/3a)
	Other relevant Statements of Attainment	AT1/2a, 2e, 3d AT2/2c, 2d, 3d AT3/2b, 3a AT4/2c, 3d AT5/2b

(Links between this unit, the Key Stage 1 Pupil Books and Book 2 are shown in the matrix on page 18 of this book.)

1 Summary and purpose

The unit as a whole

The purpose of this unit is to introduce children to reasons why people move their home (AT3/3a), with particular reference to a country in an economically developing part of Africa.

Sub-units

A village in Burkina Faso introduces Niftine Sawadogo and the village of Kalsaka, where she lives. This sub-unit also contains ideas about water supply and schooling, to link with children's direct experiences.

Finding food continues along the line of common themes, and dramatically demonstrates the effects of drought on crop yields. Ideas of soil erosion are also introduced, together with the fact that sometimes (but not all the time) people need a little help from outside; in this case in the form of Oxfam. The effects of drought on the landscape and on animal rearing, together with the role of overgrazing in desertification, are other key ideas.

The magic stones shows how much the people are doing to help themselves and how basic irrigation works are being constructed.

The firewood and water trail deals with the twin problems of finding enough fuel to burn and enough clean water for drinking, cooking, washing, etc. It also covers the extremely important aspect of women's work in Burkina Faso, especially the length and nature of the demands made on them.

Finding work deals with the pressure on many people in the Sahel to leave the countryside in search of a better life in towns and cities. The focus of the spread is the city of Abidjan in the Ivory Coast to which many people migrate. The section introduces people who have moved to Abidjan and found work, and includes examples of different types of housing, such as expensive flats and shanty dwellings. Useful comparisons can be made between this sub-unit and *Moving to the coast: Southport*.

2 Background information

The name 'Sahel' is the name given to an arid zone which runs west to east across Africa, south of the Sahara desert (see map on page 55). Sahel countries are those which fall, wholly or in part, within this zone. This is an area with very serious environmental challenges, particularly as desert conditions spread further and further south. Countries such as Chad, Niger and Burkina Faso are amongst the poorest in the world. Most people are farmers who face problems of:

- droughts, which may last several years;
- general lack of water;
- the need to move herds of cattle and goats in search of grass;
- the need to travel further to find trees which can be cut to supply wood to burn for fuel.

However, it is important not to give children the impression that the whole area is 'a problem' or even 'a disaster'. The people are not completely at the mercy of the environment. In fact, as the sub-unit shows, they have developed techniques for trapping and storing water which will allow them to continue cultivating an area with a particularly difficult climate.

The countries of the Sahel, such as Burkina Faso, are suffering 'desertification'. This is a process by which land which used to be productive (i.e. could be farmed for crops and/or animals) becomes non-productive. These areas get between 300-500mm of rainfall per year and so are certainly not deserts. However, a combination of factors is causing the land to become unproductive.

The main causes of this change are:

- droughts, which make rainfall totals unreliable from year to year;

- increasing numbers of people and animals;

- demands by large scale cash crop farming on the more productive and climatically reliable areas in the southern parts of some Sahel countries have pushed the pastoral farmers further north into the less productive areas, which cannot sustain their traditional ways of life;

- human action in overgrazing grassland areas, felling trees for fuelwood, and in allowing animals to trample extensive areas. All these activities have destroyed the vegetation and led to soil erosion and the spread of desert conditions.

The diagram shows how increasing numbers of people and animals can lead to desertification and eventual famine.

Desertification

People push the system out of balance

More people and animals

More water needed → More wells drilled → Grazing animals are pushed on to drier areas → Overgrazing → Land is stripped bare

More food needed → People grow crops on land needed for animal grazing → Crop land is overused → Crop yields fail

More fuelwood is needed → More woody plants are taken from the land → Land is stripped bare

Famine or emergency relief → Land supports fewer people and animals → Desert conditions spread (desertification)

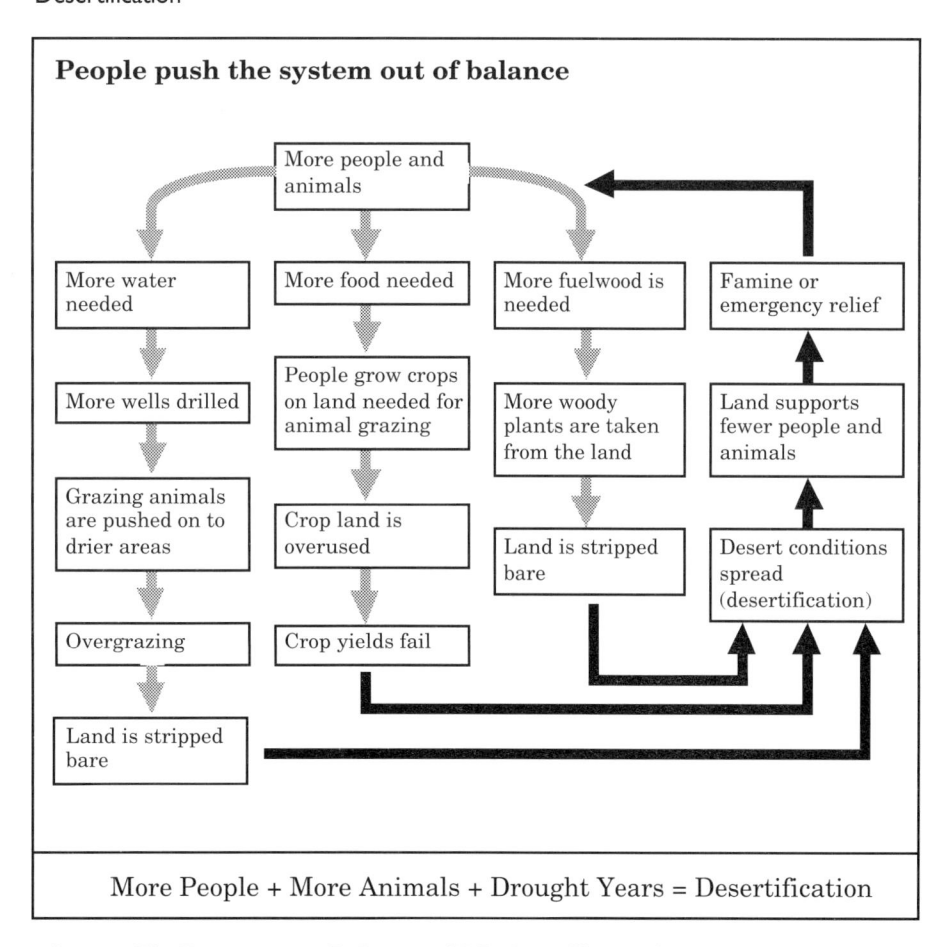

More People + More Animals + Drought Years = Desertification

(Source: *The Environment*, R. Prosser, V. Bishop, Harper Collins)

The man in picture D on page 67 of the Pupil Book is called Jean-Marie. He says, "In my father's time we never had a bad year. Millet filled all the granaries and was piled up outside the compound under the straw shelters.

"When we were boys the Savanna (woodland) was all around us. It was too thick to penetrate or cultivate. The wild animals were too many to count. There were antelope, elephants, buffaloes.

"Gradually more and more of the trees were cleared around the compounds, until each clearing met the next and created the great oneness you see now. Today the hills are bare. The only animals we see are hares. Fig trees will not grow any more. The last kapok tree fell down twenty years ago.

"When I was young, the land was fertile. You could farm the same piece of land for five years, ten years, with no fertiliser, before resting it.

"There was enough space for you to leave it for ten or twenty years before you came back to it again. Today we have to farm the same fields year after year. A piece of land that used to fill two granaries would not even fill one now; last harvest it would not even fill half a granary.

"The soil has been carried away. When I was young, you could dig a hole as deep as your body before you reached hard rock. Now in many of my fields you reach the rock if you just dig as deep as my hand.

"When I was a boy we used to have tremendous rains. It would start in the morning, and rain until the evening, and still be raining long into the night. We used to grow cotton, rice, sweet potatoes. But now it is too dry for any of these.

"Year by year the rain got less. Today when the rain starts, it continues for twenty or thirty minutes, and then stops. Sometimes we see it rain behind the mountain, but it doesn't rain here. Every year we worry whether the rain will fall or won't fall. Every year we say, 'Last year we had more than this'."

Attempting to solve desertification problems

Much time and effort is going into plans to prevent and even to reverse the effects of desertification. The main measures are:

- increasing the plant cover by reseeding areas with grass or reducing the number of grazing animals;
- planting trees for fuel and fodder;
- using drip-feed irrigation to water plant roots only;
- carrying out geological surveys of the local area to find rocks which may hold water so that new wells can be sunk;
- building earth and stone dams to catch the water in reservoirs;
- improving the soil with manures and fertilisers so that it can hold more moisture;
- planting trees as windbreaks.

Firewood

Henriette, Jean-Marie's wife, and the other women of the village of Kalsaka in Burkina Faso have to travel further and further in search of firewood. On one day they left at 7.50 a.m. and returned home at 11.30 a.m. with 23kg loads of wood on their heads. The women have to make this trip three times each week.

After fetching the firewood, the women must then fetch water before tending the crops. Wood is their only fuel for heating, cooking and light. Nine out of ten people in the rest of Africa also use wood as their main source of fuel.

Attempts to solve the firewood crisis

Tree planting is 50 times slower in the Sahel than that which is needed to replace the wood that is being chopped down. There are three main types of solution to the firewood problem:

- planting more trees to increase the supply of wood;
- making better use of existing wood by using more efficient stoves rather than open fires;
- reducing the demand for wood by providing other sources of fuel, such as bottled gas or paraffin.

Many such schemes have failed because often they did not involve local people, who felt alienated and so, for example, did not tend newly planted trees. In other cases, traditional ways of family life were centred around the open fire which provided both heat and light. New stoves provided heat only, so were not popular.

Women

Women are half the world's population, one-third of the world's official labour force, yet do two-thirds of all the world's workhours. Despite this, they receive only one-tenth of the world's income and own less than one-hundredth of the world's property.

Women, in fact, contribute much more to development than the official statistics suggest. Much of what they do is unrecorded and often their status is lower than that of men.

In Burkina Faso, women produce 95 per cent of village food supplies, fetch 90 per cent of the water and fuel and contribute 50 per cent to the process of looking after the animals – as well as looking after home and family!

Development projects do not always help women. The tasks which may be modernised are those done by men, such as ploughing. Using a tractor for ploughing actually *increases* the women's task of weeding. Similarly, women have little access to education in comparison to men, and are paid lower wages for the same task. Changes which would improve conditions for women in economically developing countries include:

- attaching greater importance to women's role in producing food;
- giving women better access to economic resources including credit;
- treating women equally in land reform, and granting them equal rights to own property;
- providing equal opportunities for education and training;
- designing technological aids to ease the burden of basic jobs;
- spending more on health services to reach women in rural areas.

Comparing the UK and Burkina Faso

The following graphs and statistics provide useful comparisons between the UK and Burkina Faso, in terms of population size, growth rate, age distribution (note the numbers under 15 in Burkina Faso) and health care.

Burkina Faso

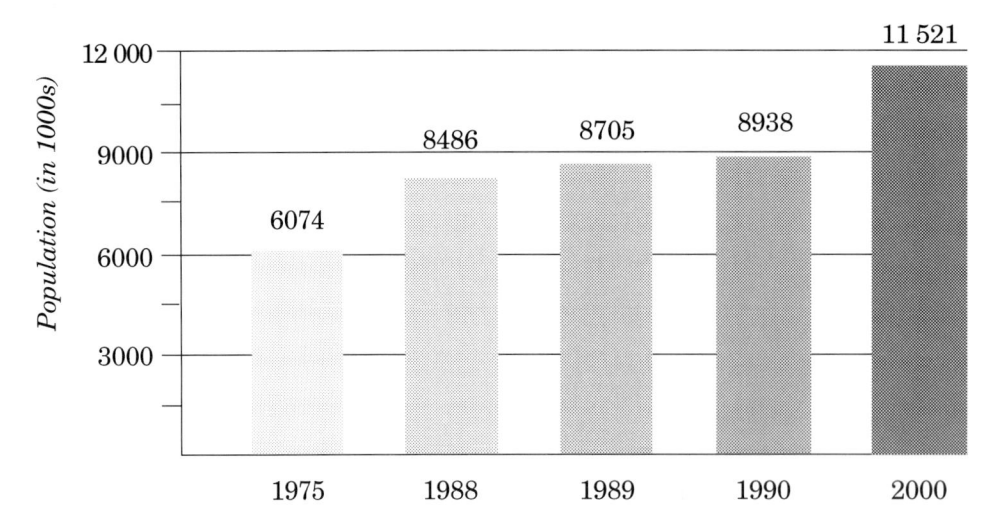

Year	Population (in 1000s)
1975	6074
1988	8486
1989	8705
1990	8938
2000	11 521

- Annual Pop'n Growth: 2.58%
- Pop'n Density: 80 inhabitants/sq mile
- Pop'n Doubling Time: 27 years

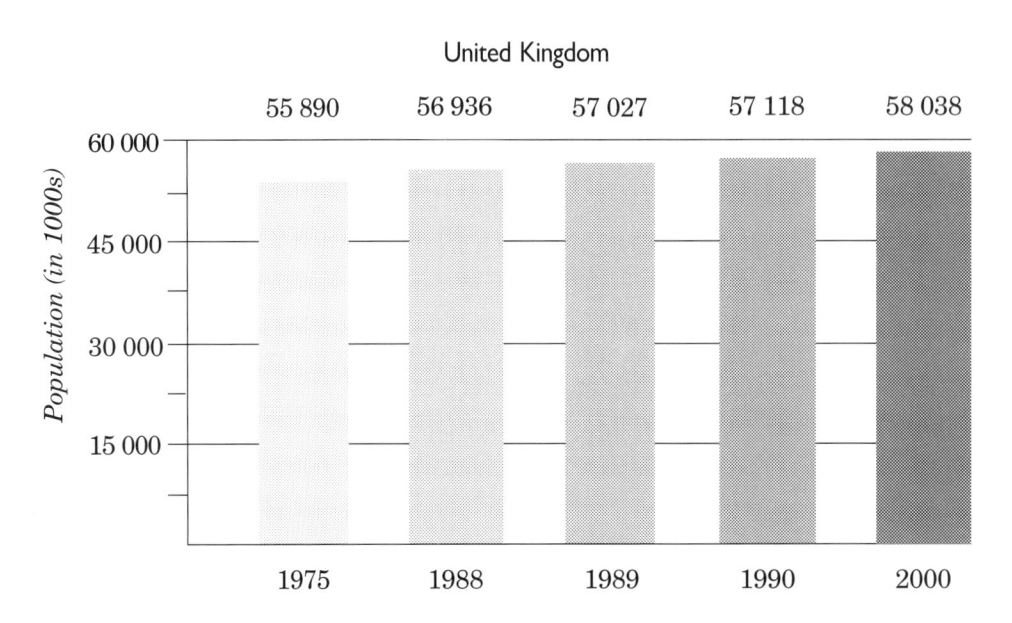

United Kingdom

Year	Population (in 1000s)
1975	55 890
1988	56 936
1989	57 027
1990	57 118
2000	58 038

- Annual Pop'n Growth: 0.16%
- Pop'n Density: 602 inhabitants/sq mile
- Pop'n Doubling Time: 434 years

Burkina Faso
Age Distribution

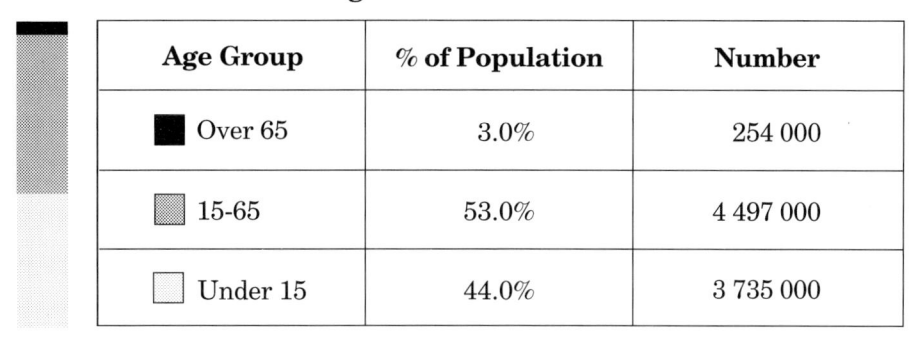

Age Group	% of Population	Number
■ Over 65	3.0%	254 000
▨ 15-65	53.0%	4 497 000
□ Under 15	44.0%	3 735 000

Total Population: 8 486 000   Literacy Rate: 7%   Urbanisation: 7.9%

United Kingdom

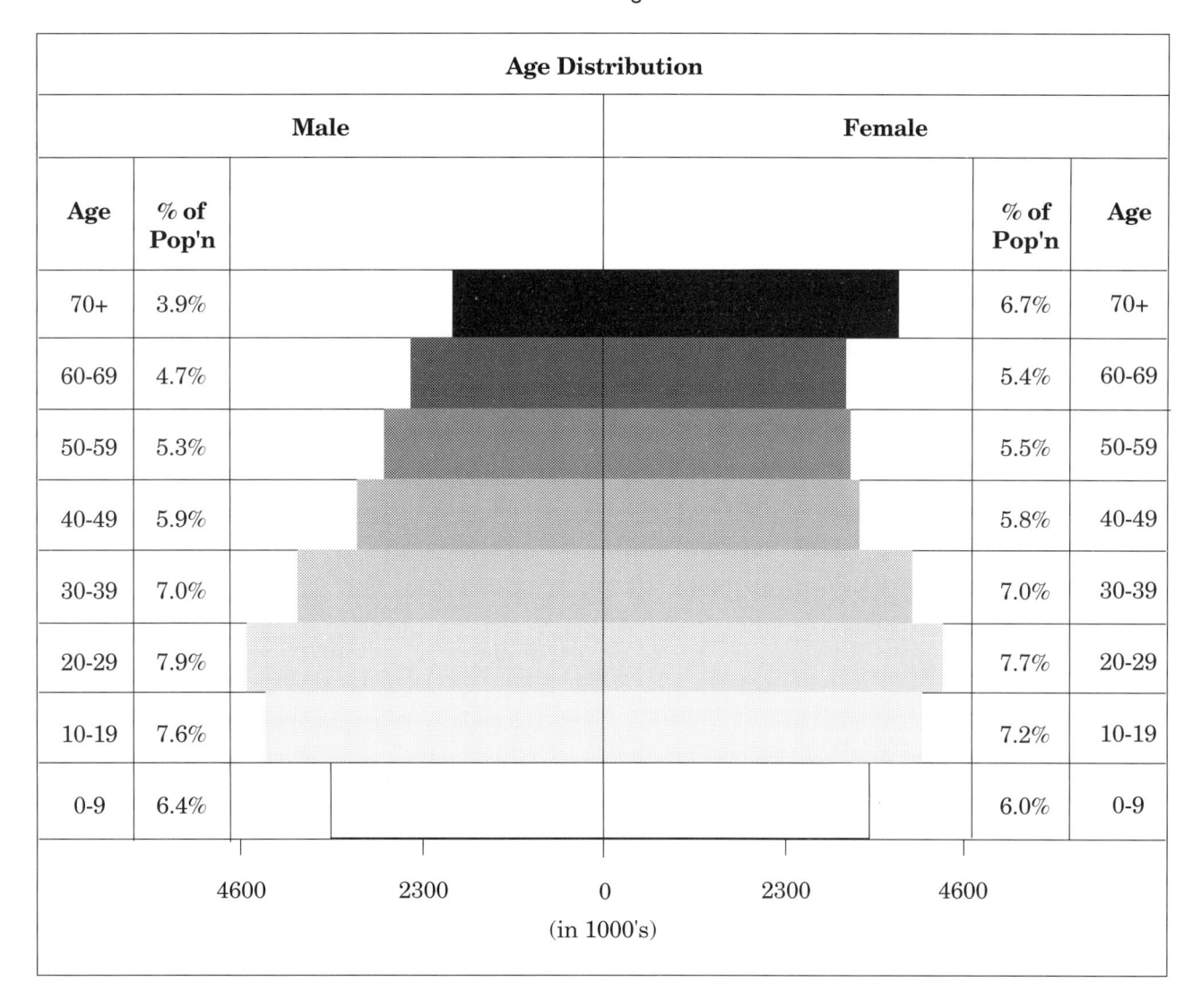

Age Distribution

Age	% of Pop'n	Male	Female	% of Pop'n	Age
70+	3.9%			6.7%	70+
60-69	4.7%			5.4%	60-69
50-59	5.3%			5.5%	50-59
40-49	5.9%			5.8%	40-49
30-39	7.0%			7.0%	30-39
20-29	7.9%			7.7%	20-29
10-19	7.6%			7.2%	10-19
0-9	6.4%			6.0%	0-9

4600   2300   0   2300   4600
(in 1000's)

- Total Population: 56 936 000
- Total Female Pop'n: 29 208 000
- Urbanisation: 91.5%
- Total Male Pop'n: 27 728 000
- Literacy Rate: 99%

United Kingdom

Health Statistics	
Life Expectancy (Male):	72.0 years
Life Expectancy (Female):	77.0 years
Crude Birth Rate:	13.3/1000
Crude Death Rate:	11.6/1000
Infant Mortality:	9.5/1000

	Number	Pop'n per
Hospitals	2262	25 171
Hospital Beds	426 594	133
Physicians	0 or N/A	0 or N/A
Dentists	8522	6681
Pharmacists	13 598	4187
Nursing Personnel	272 384	209

Burkina Faso

Health Statistics	
Life Expectancy (Male):	44.0 years
Life Expectancy (Female):	47.0 years
Crude Birth Rate:	47.8/1000
Crude Death Rate:	19.4/1000
Infant Mortality:	145.0/1000

	Number	Pop'n per
Hospitals	44	192 864
Hospital Beds	3627	2340
Physicians	127	66 819
Dentists	14	606 143
Pharmacists	46	184 478
Nursing Personnel	1927	4404

Burkina Faso

Culture & Tourism
• *Official Language*: French. • *Visa*: Required. • *Health*: Yellow fever inoculation required for entry. Tapwater not potable. Malaria suppressants, typhoid, hepatitis and cholera inoculations recommended. Swimming in lakes and streams potentially hazardous. • *Sights*: Big-game hunting, National Museum in Ougadougou, Arly and Park W game preserves. • *Climate*: Desert tropical; pronounced wet and dry seasons. Summer clothing generally suitable. Light wrap Nov-Feb. • *Currency*: CFA franc (Sept. 1989: 332.42 = $1US).
Annual Tourist Arrivals (1986): 60 000 Annual Tourist Receipts (1986): $7 000 000

Abidjan and Ivory Coast

Many people from Burkina Faso and the surrounding countries migrate to cities like Abidjan. Most large towns and cities in Africa are ports, in part due to their colonial heritage, when they were developed as points for the export of food and raw materials from the interior and imports of manufactured goods.

Ivory Coast has a population of 11.6 million people, of whom 1.8 million live in the capital, Abidjan. Population growth in Ivory Coast is rapid, and this, together with migration, has led to a massive increase in the numbers of people packed in cities like Abidjan. This growth is recent and large scale. So far, cities such as Abidjan have not been able to expand fast enough to provide basic housing and employment for their growing numbers of citizens. As the photographs in the text show, Abidjan is a city of contrasts. There are areas with broad, tree-lined streets, blocks of flats and a high-rise city centre with shops and offices. However, there are also areas of shanty towns, where people from the countryside have been forced to build their homes from any materials they can find, such as hardboard or tin sheets. They cannot afford to rent a flat or any other sort of home, so they have to build their own.

Most people who migrate to Abidjan come in search of a well-paid job. In families, the man often moves first, and brings his family later when he has saved some money and built or found a house. Unfortunately, jobs are also in short supply. With so many people looking for work, wages are low. Many people eke out an existence by providing basic services such as selling water or matches, or shining shoes. The small amounts they earn are just enough to allow them to survive in the cities, but few get rich.

3 Key ideas

1. Burkina Faso is a dry country in Africa.
2. The Sahel is an arid region along the southern edge of the Sahara desert.
3. An important task for women and children is fetching water.
4. Children in some parts of Burkina Faso can only attend school every other year, because of shortage of school accommodation.
5. Children contribute their labour to the family workload.
6. Unreliable rainfall means that the harvest varies from year to year.
7. Soil erosion is a big problem in some areas.
8. Increasing numbers of people and animals are adding to problems of drought.
9. The desert is spreading southwards.
10. Simple irrigation works using local stone can play a big part in stopping soil erosion.
11. There is a shortage of firewood and women have to travel increasing distances to find it.
12. Water supply comes from wells, pools and streams which may be contaminated.
13. Women have to walk long distances to fetch water.
14. Women perform a wide range of tasks essential to family survival.
15. Some people migrate to towns such as Abidjan.
16. Towns like Abidjan have high-rise buildings and busy streets.
17. Towns like Abidjan have both cheap and expensive flats.
18. Many people in towns like Abidjan cannot afford even simple flats, so have to build their own homes.
19. Some migrants leave their families at home, others bring them to the town.
20. Groups of home-made houses are called shanty towns.
21. Shanty towns usually have no water, electricity or sewage services.
22. People living in shanty towns often find jobs in the service sector, such as shining shoes or selling water.
23. Many people cannot find work when they migrate to the towns.

4 Questions for discussion with the children

A village in Burkina Faso
Where – does Niftine Sawadogo live?
– is Burkina Faso?
What – is the Sahel?
How – old is Niftine's baby?
Why – do children go to school every other year?

Finding food
Where – does grain go after it is picked?
What – blows away the soil?
– are sorghum and millet?
– do cattle and goats eat?
How – does the ground become bare?
Why – are the children waiting outside the school?
– do crops fail to grow?
– do goat herders have to travel a long way for food?

The magic stones
What – stops the rain washing away the soil?
How – is the soil washed away?
– do the villagers try to keep the rainwater?
Why – is the rainwater needed?
Who – builds the walls?
– carries the stones?

The firewood and water trail
What – is the wood used for?
How – is the wood carried back to the village?
– long does it take to walk to the well?
Who – helps to collect firewood?
When – does the hot season start?

On the move to find work
Where – is Abidjan?
– do rich people live?
– do people get their water from in the shanty town?
What – job does Ninsabla Sawadogo do?
– do people do who cannot afford a house?
Why – do people move to the towns?

5 Links with Copymasters

Copymaster number and title	Main focus/purpose
48 Africa	Using an atlas to complete a map
49 A village in Burkina Faso	Analysis and annotation of a picture of an African village
50 The magic stones	Describes irrigation in Burkina Faso
51 Water in Burkina Faso	Considers different uses of water in a water pool and the consequences for health
52 A woman's work	Analysis of pie graph
53 Moving from country to town	Examines causes of migration from rural to urban areas in Burkina Faso
54 Abidjan	Photo analysis of a developing city

6 Further activities

AT1/4e
1 The children could make a collection of labels from food and other products which come from Africa. These labels could be mounted on a wall map, locating the specific countries.

AT2/2c
2 A collection of newspaper cuttings relating to Africa (both news cuttings, photographs of visits by sportspeople, politicians, or royalty, together with adverts for African produce) can form the basis of work identifying countries and areas within the continent.

AT2/2d
3 Organisations such as Oxfam, Christian Aid, Save the Children, and Action Aid produce case study material on children and families in economically developing countries. Comparisons could be made with UK families in terms of food, clothing, homes, journeys, landscape, weather and work.

AT2/2d
4 Children can draw circular diagrams similar to the one on page 75 for themselves and their parents, to show how their day is divided up. Similarities and differences can then be highlighted.

AT5/4c
5 A survey of the school grounds can often identify places where the children's feet trample the ground. This area can be studied to identify why it has become trampled, e.g. as a short cut, and how the plants change if trampling continues. Plans could also be made for improvements to the area, to revive (or replant) the site and to avoid similar problems in the future.

AT3/3b
6 Children can carry out simple experiments, pouring cans of water over a mound of loose earth. The water will quickly form channels in the mound, whose height will be reduced as more and more of the soil is washed to the base of the mound. Simple ideas of soil erosion by water can be developed, together with different approaches to halting it, e.g. building barriers with stones across the slope.

AT5/4a	7	A daily record of how much water each child in the class uses each day for different purposes (e.g. drinking, using the toilet, washing, cleaning teeth) can form the basis for comparisons with water use in the village (see page 73).
AT2/3d	8	The photographs of Abidjan (pages 76-80) can form the basis of work identifying similarities and differences with UK cities (e.g. houses, roads, flats, offices, bridges, trees).
AT4/3a	9	Children can use the photographs on page 78 to write speech bubbles of what they think those people might be saying about their life and work.

Although only geography ATs have been listed above, many of the activities provide opportunities for developing knowledge and skills in other subject areas, as well as cross-curricular elements (see 'Cross-curricular elements' on page 95).

Section 3:

Oliver and Boyd Geography and the National Curriculum

Geography at Key Stage 2

'Geography explores the relationship between the Earth and its people through the study of place, space *and* environment. *Geographers ask the questions* Where? *and* What?; *also* How? *and* Why?'

(Final Report of the National Curriculum Geography Working Party, June 1990.)

Where to start?

Children at Key Stage 2 will have a wide range of geographical experiences, both formal and informal. They will have developed a view of the world, based on first hand experiences in the home locality together with glimpses of the wider world through television, picture books and comics. Increasingly, they will have benefited from an introduction to geographical ideas, skills and knowledge at Key Stage 1. A good school geography programme aims to build on these various experiences and to provide a framework to meet children's growing curiosity about places in the world. In this context, some Pupil Books from *Oliver and Boyd Geography* Key Stage 1, namely – *Living in Hong Kong*, *Living on Islands*, *Living in the Mountains*, *Hot Places* and *Cold Places*, address levels 2/3 in the Attainment Targets, and Book 1 of the Key Stage 2 materials develops and extends those same levels, with a greater emphasis on level 3 (see pages 11/18).

What do the Statutory Orders for Geography say?

The Statutory Orders for Geography in the National Curriculum identify five Attainment Targets.

Attainment Targets

AT1 Geographical skills

AT2 Knowledge and understanding of places

AT3 Physical geography

AT4 Human geography

AT5 Environmental geography

Summary of Attainment Targets

Geographical skills cover the use of maps and the development of fieldwork techniques to investigate the environment. Enquiry should also form an important part of pupils' work (see page 78).

Knowledge and understanding of places concerns the knowledge children need of places, both local and distant. This includes ideas of what makes a particular place distinctive (see *In the Neighbourhood*) as well as similarities and differences between places and how the themes and issues can be observed in the context of particular places (see *People on the Move* in Pupil Book 1).

Physical geography concentrates on:

- weather (both locally and in other parts of the world);
- water in the environment; and
- landscape features such as hills and valleys, rocks and soil.

Human geography is about:
- people (population);
- places to live (settlements);
- getting around (communications and movements);
- work (economic activities); and
- leisure.

Environmental geography is about:
- resources (such as soil, water, oil);
- how people use and abuse resources;
- why environments can easily be damaged; and
- why we need to protect some special environments.

Programme of Study for Key Stage 2: Levels 2 to 5

Geographical skills

1 Enquiry should form an important part of pupil's work in Key Stage 2. It should take account of pupils' interests, experience and capabilities, and lead to investigations based on fieldwork and classroom activities. Pupils should develop their geographical skills through studying places and geographical themes. They should be given opportunities to use information technology (IT).

2 Pupils should be taught to:

- observe geographical features and conditions using simple instruments, for example, tape measures, rain gauges, clinometers, stopwatches, wind speed gauges, weather vanes, thermometers, callipers and compasses, to make measurements;

- select relevant information from a variety of sources, for example, visitors, photographs, maps, charts, documents, atlases, globes, videos, TV and radio programmes, computer databases, books, newspapers.

3 Pupils should be taught to:

- use pictures and photographs to identify features, for example, homes, railways, rivers, hills, and to find out about places; describe what they see using geographical terms;

- interpret symbols, measure direction and distance, follow routes and describe the location of places using maps;

- make representations of real or imaginary places; make and use maps of routes, and sketch maps of small areas showing the main features and using symbols with keys;

- use the eight points of the compass;

- determine the straight line distance between two points on a map;

- locate their position and identify features outside the classroom using a large-scale map;

- identify features on vertical aerial photographs, for example, railway lines, rivers and roads, and match them to a map;

- use maps to find out where features are located and where activities take place;
- find information in an atlas using the index and contents pages;
- measure and record the weather using direct observation and simple equipment.

4 Pupils working towards level 5 should be taught to:

- use conventional 1:50,000 or 1:25,000 Ordnance Survey map symbols with the aid of a key;
- follow a route on an Ordnance Survey map and describe what would be seen;
- use six-figure grid references to locate features on a map;
- interpret relief maps;
- extract information from distribution patterns shown on maps;
- use a map to identify features they have seen;
- use latitude and longitude to locate places on atlas maps;
- recognise that a globe can be represented as a flat surface

Places and themes

Places

5 Pupils should develop their knowledge and understanding about places and themes. Pupils should be taught how to acquire information and develop skills that enable them to interpret and make sense of the knowledge gained.

6 Pupils should learn to identify, on globes and maps, local places, places that are frequently in the news, and places they are studying. They should be taught to:

- identify on globes or maps the points of reference specified on Maps A and C and on Maps B and D at the end of the programmes of study;
- name and locate on a map the constituent countries of the United Kingdom and mark on a map of the British Isles approximately where they live.

7 Pupils working towards level 5 should be taught to:

- identify on globes or maps the points of reference specified on Maps E and F at the end of the programmes of study.

8 During Key Stage 2 pupils should study:

	Levels			
Localities	2	3	4	
the local area	•	•	•	
a contrasting area in the UK	•	•	•	
a locality in an economically developing country	•	•	•	•
a locality in a European Community country outside the UK				•
Regions				
Home region			•	•

The definition of the home region should be determined by the pupils' teachers, taking into account the location of the school and the need to encompass an area which is substantial either in area or population.

Local area 9 Pupils should study their local area. They should be taught to:

- investigate the use of land and buildings in the local area, and use correct geographical vocabulary to identify types of landscape features and industrial and leisure activities which they have observed in the local area;.

- observe and suggest reasons for the relationships between land-use, buildings and human activities in the local area;

- suggest reasons for the location of economic activities in the local area and offer reasons for the location of specified activities in the area.

Home region 10 Pupils should be taught:

- that their own locality can be considered as part of a region;

- the geographical features of the home region.

11 Pupils working towards level 5 should be taught:

- how the main features of the home region are inter-related.

Other localities 12 Pupils should study a contrasting locality in the United Kingdom and a locality in an economically developing country. They should be taught:

- to investigate features of other localities, for example, through looking at holiday postcards and photographs, and how these features might affect people's lives;

- to describe the features and occupations of the other localities studied and compare them with those of the local area;

- to identify and describe similarities and differences between their local area and other localities;

- how the localities studied have changed as a result of human actions;

- to investigate recent or proposed changes in a locality;

- to examine the impact of landscape, weather and wealth on the lives of people in a locality in an economically developing country.

13 Pupils working towards level 5 should be taught:

- how the occupations, land-use and settlement patterns of both a locality in an economically developing country and a locality in a European Community country outside the United Kingdom are related to that area's environment and location.

Physical geography 14 Pupils should be taught:

- to identify and describe landscape features, for example, a river, hill, valley, lake, beach, with which they are familiar;

- how site conditions can influence surface temperatures and affect wind speed and direction, and the effect of different surfaces and slopes on rainwater when it reaches the ground;

- the nature and effects of earthquakes and volcanic eruptions, and how the latter produce craters, cones and lava flows;

- to identify water in different forms;

- that rivers have sources, channels, tributaries, and mouths, that they receive water from a wide area, and that most eventually flow into a lake or the sea;

- that rivers, waves, winds and glaciers erode, transport and deposit materials;

- to recognise seasonal weather patterns;
- about weather conditions in different parts of the world, for example, in polar, temperate, tropical desert and tropical forest regions;
- to investigate and compare the colour, texture and organic content of different types of soil.

15 Pupils working towards level 5 should be taught:

- the effects of frost action, chemical and biological weathering, for example, on roads and buildings, and the distinction between weathering and erosion;
- to examine the global distribution of earthquakes and volcanoes and how this relates to the boundaries of the crustal plates;
- the causes and effects of river floods and methods used to reduce floodrisk;
- the difference between weather and climate;
- seasonal patterns of temperature and rainfall over the British Isles.

Human geography   16 Pupils should be taught:

- why some parts of the world contain very few people while the other parts are densely populated;
- to investigate why people make journeys of different lengths, why different means of transport may be used for different purposes and how people and goods transfer from one means of transport to another;
- why people move homes, for example, change of employment, retirement, marriage, to find a bigger or smaller home or a more attractive location, emigration, famine, war;
- to study a route linking two places and understand why roads and railways do not always take the shortest route between the places they link;
- that most homes are part of a settlement and that settlements vary in size; how the functions and origins of settlements may be revealed by their current features;
- to study the layout and functions of a small settlement, or part of a larger settlement, and evaluate the impact of any recent or current changes;
- how goods and services needed by the community are provided;
- how land is used in different ways, for example, farming, buildings, leisure, manufacturing industry; the reasons for different uses of land and for the location of different types of economic activities, for example, sources of power, labour, raw materials, the transport network, the location of the purchaser of the services or goods; why different amounts of land are required for different purposes; and to study a particular issue which demonstrates how conflicts can arise due to competition over the use of land.

17 Pupils working towards level 5 should be taught:

- to examine and seek reasons for changes in the population size of regions and countries;
- to compare different transport networks and the effects of changes in these networks;

- reasons for the location and growth of individual settlements and the benefits and problems accompanying growth;
- why economic activities may develop in particular locations;
- to investigate types and patterns of land-use in farming, manufacturing industry and the retail industry.

Environmental geography

18 Pupils should be taught:

- ways of extracting materials from the environment and how the extraction of natural resources affects environments, for example, quarries, mining;
- the differences between manufactured goods and natural resources;
- about fresh water sources and means of ensuring a reliable supply;
- to identify activities which have changed the environment; to consider ways in which they can improve their own environment; and about activities intended to improve the local environment or a place they have visited;
- ways in which people look after and improve the environment; some of the ways in which damaged environments can be restored and damage prevented; and to consider whether some types of environment need special protection.

19 Pupils working towards level 5 should be taught:

- the differences between renewable and non-renewable resources;
- why rivers, lakes and seas are vulnerable to pollution and to investigate ways in which pollution problems have been addressed.

What do the Statutory Orders mean?

The Attainment Targets define the major elements of geography, but when teachers plan their work these elements should not be seen in isolation, nor should they be used as a rigid framework for planning. The Programme of Study for Key Stage 2 (see pages 00-00) is the most appropriate basis for planning, with Statements of Attainment being used as a checklist for the purposes of assessment.

The following diagram shows how work on skills, places and themes can be combined in a variety of ways:

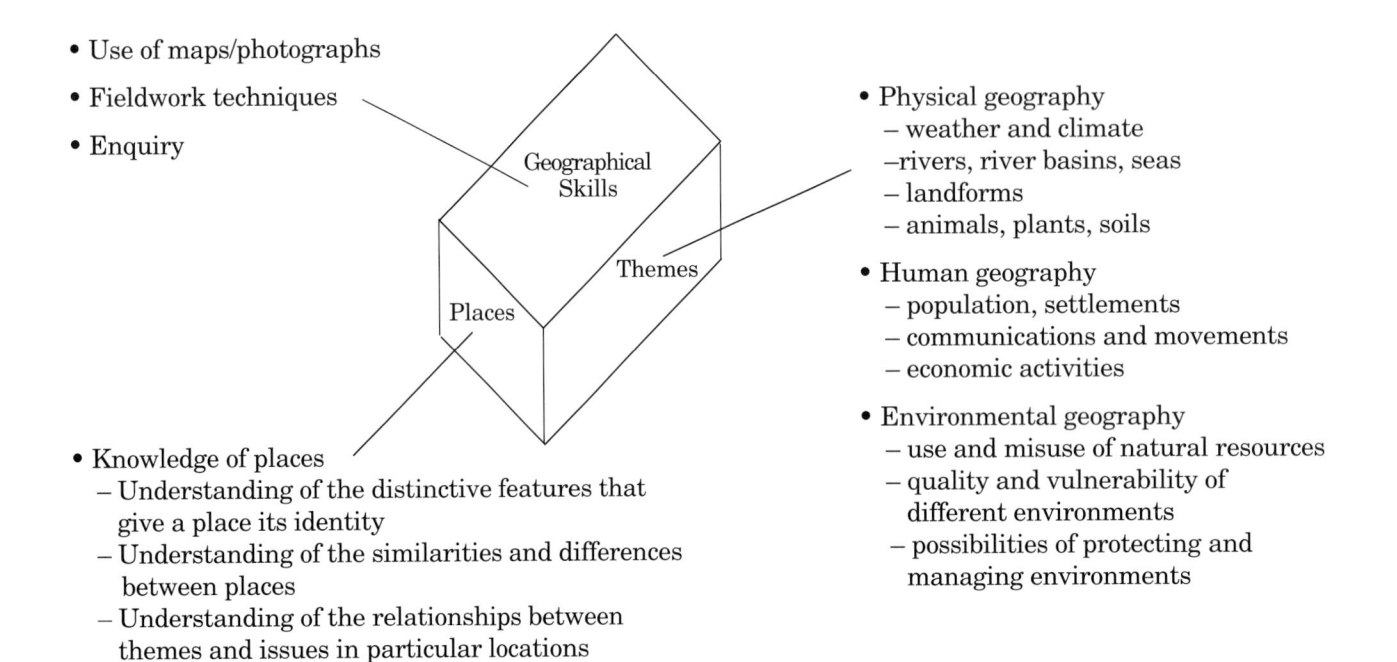

- Use of maps/photographs
- Fieldwork techniques
- Enquiry

Geographical Skills

Themes

Places

- Physical geography
  - weather and climate
  - rivers, river basins, seas
  - landforms
  - animals, plants, soils

- Human geography
  - population, settlements
  - communications and movements
  - economic activities

- Environmental geography
  - use and misuse of natural resources
  - quality and vulnerability of different environments
  - possibilities of protecting and managing environments

- Knowledge of places
  - Understanding of the distinctive features that give a place its identity
  - Understanding of the similarities and differences between places
  - Understanding of the relationships between themes and issues in particular locations

Each component in *Oliver and Boyd Geography* combines aspects of the Attainment Targets in this way. Pupils are encouraged to enquire about places and themes as well as developing a range of geographical skills (see the following example from Pupil Book 1, *People on the Move*).

People on the Move

Moving to the coast: Southport
Welcome to Southport!

The card in A was sent to Mr and Mrs Jennings when Mr Jennings retired from work.

Most people work until they are 60 or 65 years old. When they retire, they have more time to rest and to do the things they enjoy.

Look at these photographs. What can retired people do in Southport?

Some people move house when they retire. They may go to live in seaside resorts. Southport is a seaside resort. Mr and Mrs Jennings moved there from Preston when they retired.

Look at B.
1a How can you tell that Southport is a seaside resort?
1b What would you do if you visited Southport?

Look at C, D, E and F.
2a Write a label for each photograph to say what it shows.
2b There are lots of seats and benches in the streets and parks in Southport. Why do you think there are so many?
2c Why is Southport a good place for older people to live?

- Studying photographs
- Using geographical vocabulary
- Using maps
- Studying aerial photographs
- Studying climate graphs
- Enquiry methods

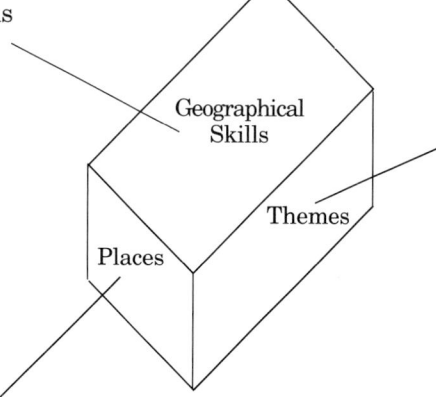

Geographical Skills

Themes

Places

Southport UK

The Sahel in Africa

Life in an economically developing country

- Reasons why people move homes, e.g. retirement, search for a job
- Amenities for retirement
- Different types of transport
- Weather records
- Weather and climate in the Sahel
- Reasons why there are many people in some places and few in others
- Farming and weather
- Effects of drought, farming and fuelwood cutting on the environment
- Attempts to repair environmental destruction
- Water supply - problems and prospects
- Housing types
- Different kinds of work in the developing world

Where does geography fit in the school curriculum?

Some of the geography programme for children at Key Stage 2 will continue to be delivered through child-centred, integrated programmes, but geography at Key Stage 2 is moving away from the immediate, the individual and the local, towards the collective and more 'distant' (both within the UK and in an economically developing country). The core of each unit of study remains the locality and this is reflected in the structure of *Oliver and Boyd Geography*, where in Pupil Book 1 the first two units are studies of school localities in Inverness and Coventry.

Basic ideas are developed in Book 1 of the Key Stage 2 series which both build on work in the Key Stage 1 material and are revisited in later books of the Key Stage 2 series. For example, the idea of routes is developed in the Key Stage 1 Pupil Books *Going to School* and *Living in Hong Kong*, and this is taken a stage further in the first sub-unit of Book 1 and in several other units in Book 1 and Book 2.

Similarly, the idea of weather is developed in the Key Stage 1 Pupil Books *Weather*, *Hot Places* and *Cold Places*. This theme is expanded in the unit on the Sahel in Book 1 and again in the units entitled *Weather and Farming* and *An Indian City: Delhi* in Book 2. (See 'Progression Pathways' matrix on page 18.)

What should teachers be trying to do in geography at Key Stage 2?

Some key aims for teachers in developing geographical ideas in the primary years are as follows:

(a) 'to stimulate pupils' interest in their surroundings and the variety of physical and human conditions on the Earth's surface;

(b) 'to foster their sense of wonder at the beauty of the world around them;

(c) 'to help them to develop an informed concern about the quality of the environment and the future of the human habitat; and

(d) 'thereby enhance their sense of responsibility for the care of the Earth and its peoples.'

(Final Report of the National Curriculum Geography Working Party, June 1990.)

Geography and enquiry

'Enquiry should form an important part of pupils' work in Key Stage 2. It should take account of pupils' interests, experience and capabilities, and lead to investigations based on fieldwork and classroom activities. Pupils should develop their geographical skills through studying places and geographical themes. They should be given opportunities to use information technology (IT).' (Programme of Study for Key Stage 2, Statutory Orders for Geography.)

Enquiry is an important part of all geographical teaching and learning. The term 'enquiry' is not always fully understood, however. Enquiry is the process of encouraging children to ask questions and to devise ways of exploring such questions.

The distinctive feature of geographical enquiry is the concern with places – both near and far – and the kinds of questions we ask about those places. Some of the key questions are listed below, together with subsidiary questions arising from the main focus. Teachers employing these questions in relation to the places and themes they are studying with their children will be taking part in geographical enquiry.

Enquiry: Questions to ask about Places (After R. Carter)

Questions to ask in Geography	Examples of consequent activities
What do I already know about this place? What will I expect to find? What will it be like? What do I think about it?	**Speculating** Drawing upon the child's previous experience. Perceptions culled from direct and indirect experiences. Imaginative work.
Where is it? What does it look like? Are there many or few people? What is it like to live there? What's the weather like? Are there many visitors? What is distinctive about it?	**Describing** Locating, describing, collecting and sorting information. Classifying, using books, maps, atlas, globe, artefacts, people. Fieldwork.
Why is it like it is? Why is it where it is? How did it get like this? Why did it happen? How can we explain it? How is life affected by the place – or its location? How have people used or modified the place? How does it link with other places? Why is it similar to/different from where we live?	**Explaining** Connections between factors (e.g. climate and farming). Relationship between people and environments. Connections between places. Factors which explain. Bringing together evidence from a variety of sources to seek explanations. Making comparisons. Reasoning.
How is it changing? How might things change? With what impact? What decisions will be made? Who will decide? Who will gain? or lose? What are the alternatives? Will the changes bring improvement? For whom?	**Predicting** Using newspapers, magazines, TV programmes and videos to identify change or possible change. Looking at current issues, questions or conflicts. Simulation games. Computer prediction models.
What would it feel like to be here? What are the views of the people who live here? What do others think and feel about it? What do I think and feel about it? What can I do?	**Responding** Imaginative work. Curiosity – empathy. Use of literature and television. Account of journeys. Diaries. Photographs. Letters from distant places. Making pictures. Role play.

Questions such as those listed below, when applied to any place and its people, will lead children into a range of worthwhile activities which, taken in combination, will enhance their sense of place.

Children need not necessarily apply all questions to every area of study. Younger children may be more concerned with aspects of where places are and what they are like. However, over time, children should be encouraged to pursue questions across the full range, thus leading them into a range of activities.

Some questions are easier to respond to than others. The teacher's role may be that of facilitator and manager of learning to enable pupils to seek answers. Some questions are speculative, some require a personal response. Frequently, there is no correct answer to a question – *the enquiry approach and the process of seeking solutions will often be as important as the answers arrived at.*

Pursuing a range of questions about places and people will take children beyond the basic requirements for teaching and assessing the National Curriculum, by developing curiosity and providing opportunities for them to develop and explore their own attitudes and values, as well as acquiring skills and knowledge.

Values and attitudes in geography

Geography is a powerful vehicle for developing attitudes and values. Most geographical enquiries offer opportunities for children to explore and clarify their own values and attitudes, as well as those of other people. The teacher's role is one of selecting themes and topics which are most relevant to particular values and attitudes, then designing activities which will help children to make reasoned judgements.

The most significant values and attitudes relating to geography are as follows:

- curiosity, fostered through the encouragement of questions and enquiry;
- open-mindedness, fostered through discussions of alternative viewpoints, solutions and perceptions;
- a critical approach to information, fostered through fieldwork and other data collection, processing and analysis activities;
- justice and fairness, fostered through considerations of different approaches to similar problems;
- a concern for the quality of the environment, fostered through examination of possible threats to environments, both local and global;
- a commitment to improving the environment, fostered through considerations of how far individual actions can lead to environmental improvements.

Children should be encouraged to consider that people have the power to change their environment in both positive and negative ways.

Developing mapwork skills using *Oliver and Boyd Geography*

The development of map reading skills is a fundamental part of geography and the Pupil Books and Copymasters in *Oliver and Boyd Geography* provide numerous resources and related activities to support this development.

The grid below shows the elements of map reading that are covered by the Copymasters for Key Stage 1, and by Copymasters 1 for Key Stage 2. Elements such as scale and contours which are applicable at later levels and with older children are developed in later sets of Copymasters and are shown in mapwork grids in the relevant Teacher's Books.

The mapwork activities are designed to put mapwork into contexts which are meaningful and interesting, so children should find them both relevant and fun to do. There is a clear progression through the Copymasters so the children can move through them at their own pace and level. The grid below identifies the key mapping skills and lists the masters which develop them. Thus, the teacher can sort them into a progressive sequence and hand them out to children as appropriate to their own progress.

The Pupil Books, particularly those for Key Stage 2, contain numerous maps which have been carefully designed to introduce different features and styles at the appropriate level. Thus, three-dimensional pictorial maps predominate in Books 1 and 2, scales are not introduced until Book 2, and four-figure coordinates do not appear until Book 3.

There are several mapwork activities in the Pupil Books which encourage children to interrogate the maps provided. Simplified versions of some of these are also reproduced in the related Copymasters. The expendable nature of the Copymasters enables pupils to answer map-related questions on the masters themselves, and also to add or colour in various features on the maps. For example, tasks such as route planning are better suited to the copymaster format, as are activities which involve cutting and pasting pictures in sequence.

The Copymasters and Pupil Books are therefore mutually reinforcing, with the former both supplementing and extending the range of mapping activities offered by the Pupil Books.

Developing mapwork skills through the Copymasters

Main elements of mapwork	Key Stage 1 Copymasters	Key Stage 2 Copymasters 1
Location (Language of Location)	7, 21, 22, 63, 64	
Introducing symbols	1, 30, 31, 32, 33	9, 10, 19
Plan view	13, 14, 19, 45, 46, 59, 61	3, 4, 5, 6, 8, 10, 15, 16, 17, 32, 44, 45, 47
Direction	5, 21, 23, 24, 44, 48	40
Distance and scale	Not applicable	8, 47
Routes	46, 61, 62	5, 7, 15, 16, 25, 27, 30
Coordinates	36, 37	11, 27, 44

Using photographs in Oliver and Boyd Geography

It is important to use a range and variety of photographs with children as a key part of their geographical education, and *Oliver and Boyd Geography* provides for this.

There are numerous activities in the Pupil Books which help to develop photo interpretation skills, but even more value can be extracted from the resources if the following general points and principles are observed:

- children rarely see what we see in photographs;
- children tend to glance quickly at the whole photograph, and acquire only a very general impression of what it contains;
- the details in a photograph, such as key features in the background, or different groups in the foreground, are missed by many children.

Ways of using photographs with children

Visual images are similar to written images in that the teacher needs to help children to understand how to 'read' them, in the same way that they help children to read a book. The following activities should help teachers to achieve this:

- ask the children to devise as many questions as possible about a particular photograph, e.g. what is in the foreground? What is in the background? What do you think the people might be saying? What do you think the people might be thinking? Where was the photograph taken? What time of day is it? What was the weather like? Pupils can then discuss their questions with the teacher, focusing attention on the key features of the photograph;

- children may be asked what they think is to the immediate left or right of the subject shown in a photograph. This requires detailed examination of all parts of the picture before suggestions can be considered;

- children may be asked what happened just before or just after the photograph was taken. Again, detailed scrutiny of the image will be necessary prior to discussion.

- For photographs showing people, place a sheet of acetate over the photograph and ask the children to draw and write into speech bubbles the things the people might be saying. For example, for photo H on Page 78 of Pupil Book 1, the boy on the left might be saying, "Who is this person taking the photograph?" One of the persons crouched down could be asking, "Why is he/she taking a photograph?", and the other, "I wish they would hurry up, I am getting cramp." The person on the extreme right might say, "I wish we could live in a better house," and so on.

- One child in a group could be asked to select a photograph from a section of the Pupil Book, but not to tell the rest which photograph it is. The others in the group then have to ask questions until they can locate the correct picture.

- Children can work in pairs, one child could cover up part of one photograph and the other has to guess what the complete picture shows, using evidence such as facial expression, dress, landscape, body position, etc.

- Children can work in pairs, each child with a different picture from the same sub-unit or double spread in the Pupil Book. They study the pictures for 30 seconds, then they close the book. They then take it in turns to describe their picture to their partner. Then together they study the photographs, and consider things such as, What was left out? How does the picture differ from the partner's image? What things were invented?

- Children can look through all the photographs in one sub-unit of the Pupil Book for one minute. They then close the book and have to list and describe all the photographs they can remember.

- Children working in pairs can be asked to devise captions for particular photographs. Can different groups devise different captions for the same photograph? How do the words affect our view of the photograph?

Looking for hidden 'values' in photographs

Not only do children need help in 'reading' photographs, they also need help in understanding that photographs have been selected by someone, and that this selection can be for different purposes. It is useful, therefore, to encourage children to take their own photographs of the school and its immediate environment. A large display of such photographs can then be produced and 6 shots chosen which could best represent the neighbourhood to children from another part of the country. Discussion of which photographs to select raises issues such as which set of pictures gives a very positive image of the area (all the best bits) or a very negative image (all the worst spots). This type of activity will encourage children to question photographs and begin to frame questions such as, Is it really like that? This is particularly important when studying photographs of more distant places, such as the Sahel.

Progression in the use of different types of photographs

Photographs used in geographical work fall into three main categories: ground views, oblique views and vertical views. In the *Oliver and Boyd Geography* Key Stage 2 Pupil Books, these have been introduced at different points and in a sequence which relates to the average child's stage of development.

1 Ground level views of buildings, people, and general scenes predominate in Book 1. These can be understood by most children, and can form the basis for useful discussions and simple analysis.

2 Oblique aerial views are also introduced in Book 1, but in small numbers. These are shots of places taken as if from a tall building, looking down and across. The angle of the shot varies, so children will see how the image of places can change, depending on the viewpoint.

3 Oblique views taken from an aeroplane come next in level of difficulty. These need careful study in order to pick out roads, houses, trees, cars, and other key features. Labels have been added to some of these photographs in the Pupil Books, to help pupils to identify such features.

4 Vertical air photographs are not introduced until Book 3 (level 4). Because these show the layout of places, with buildings etc. in plan view, they provide a useful introduction to two-dimensional plans and maps, and, initially, are accompanied by maps of the same area with land-use and other features described through a key.

Planning work with a geographical content

The following procedure will enable teachers to plan their work effectively to include a geographical dimension based on the *Oliver and Boyd Geography* materials.

1. Select your programme of content for the Key Stage, drawing from the Programme of Study, the pupils' and your own interests, and resources in the school. Consider the need for progression, sequence and continuity.

2. For each unit of work, organise the progress through a series of key enquiry questions such as those in Section 2 of this Teacher's Book.

3. Develop appropriate activities to pursue these questions (see Section 2).

4. Relate the activities to ATs and levels statements (see Section 2).

5. Identify what you will assess from the programme and how you will assess it.

Remember that future geographical work, like all good early years teaching, will retain the best elements of present practice, especially:

Active learning
Geography provides a myriad of opportunities for active learning, where children can take a key role, not least in empathising about what it might be like to live elsewhere.

Discovery
Children are naturally curious about the world in which they live. The more children are encouraged to find out about the world using *Oliver and Boyd Geography*, the greater will be the effective learning.

The importance of skills and knowledge
Adopting the enquiry approach will enable children to develop and practise existing skills as well as acquiring new ones. They will learn about themselves, their locality and other localities and people.

Using stimuli such as stories, poems and music
Many stories and poems traditionally used with Key Stage 2 children have a geographical dimension which can be developed and made explicit. A list of other suitable titles is given in Appendix 2. Pictures, poems, and music can also make valuable starting points for work on topics such as weather, shops, mining and migration.

Good practice

A good geography topic will:

- develop locational knowledge – know where places are;
- develop basic skills in mapwork;
- encourage learning outside the classroom as well as inside;
- encourage children to ask geographical questions;
- introduce children to places and people both near and far;

- challenge children's stereotypes of other people and places and encourage empathy;
- provide a framework within which children will be able to place geographical knowledge;
- make links with work in other curricular areas such as maths, English, history, science;
- increase children's understanding of what geographers study;
- involve the children actively in learning;
- stimulate children's interest and curiosity;
- be enjoyable and fun.

Section 4:

Assessment, Recording, Cross-curricular elements and Information Technology (IT)

Assessing and recording pupil progress

By the end of Key Stage 2, teachers will need to be in a position to do the following:

- report individual and class achievements in the geography curriculum;
- contribute evidence and assessment to statements relating to cross-curricular themes, skills and dimensions;
- identify individual progress;
- be able to contribute comments on pupils' wider achievements.

Depending on the audience (i.e. parents, governors, LEA), the above may be needed separately, or in combination.

Hence, although there will not be statutory assessment in geography by Standard Assessment Tasks (SATs) at the end of Key Stage 2, non-statutory SATs will be available for use in assessing individual progress and learning problems and planning a variety of different types of pupil activities. The materials in *Oliver and Boyd Geography* – particularly the Copymasters and Section 2 of this book – provide considerable support for these needs. The Copymasters each provide space for pupils to write in their names, and the majority invite responses to be made on the sheets themselves, thus providing a ready-made record of the pupil's progress and understanding of a wide range of Statements of Attainment (see matrix on pages 16,17).

In addition, the NCC and CCW Geography Non-Statutory Guidance document offers a checklist on general assessment procedures. During 1992, the NCC will also be producing INSET materials for primary geography.

What should an eleven-year-old be able to do in geography?

The following list provides examples of the types of achievement for a typical 11 year-old, based on the Programme of Study for Key Stage 2 (see pages 71 – 75 for the full Programme). Other elements from the Programme of Study can, of course, be added to this selection.

At the end of Key Stage 2, children aged 11 should be able to:

- respond to geographical questions, such as 'Where is this place?' 'What is it like?' 'Why is it like this?' 'How is this place changing?' 'What would it be like to live there?';
- use maps, photographs (including oblique and vertical air photographs) and pictures of places both local and distant;
- describe in oral, map, pictorial or written form the features of the local area, a contrasting UK locality, a locality in an economically developing country, and the home region (plus an EC locality at level 5);
- identify water in its different forms, describe seasonal weather patterns in the UK and other parts of the world, and describe the work of rivers, wind and ice;
- describe the effects of volcanoes and earthquakes;
- describe the homes, buildings, services, work, leisure and landscape of the local area and a locality in an economically developing country;
- explain why people move homes;
- describe the effects of extracting raw materials on environments and attempts to improve environments.

Assessment, Recording, Cross-curricular elements and Information Technology (IT)

Recording pupil progress

Any system of recording must:

- be relatively simple to carry out;
- be simple to complete;
- tell another reader something meaningful about individual achievements (especially parents);
- be clearly related to the National Curriculum;
- be designed to emphasise positive pupil achievements.

Two possibilities are:

1 A class record
The sample record sheet on page 91 shows one way in which teachers could maintain a class record on one sheet. As with all such vehicles, it cannot provide a great deal of information about the achievements of individual children, but it is a useful document for planning future work. Such a class record does help to highlight those Attainment Targets which may have been neglected in earlier work, and thus allow topics to be chosen which will encourage activities in the neglected areas.

2 Curriculum mapping
The matrix on page 92 shows an approach based on cross-curricular topic planning familiar to many teachers. It enables pupil activities to be mapped across both core and foundation subjects, and is again useful in highlighting 'gaps' in pupil experience. (This example comes from *A Sense of History, Key Stage 1 Teacher's Book*, Longman, 1991).

3 Recording individual pupil progress
An example of how a record of individual pupil progress may be compiled is given on page 93. This relates to the sub-unit, On the move in the Sahel in Pupil Book 1. A blank record sheet is also provided on page 94.

Unit of work: The Sahel
At the planning stage the teacher may identify what skills, places and themes will be covered by the Sahel theme (and at what levels). The initial planning diagram may look like this:

- Analysis of photographs
- Analysis of oblique air photographs

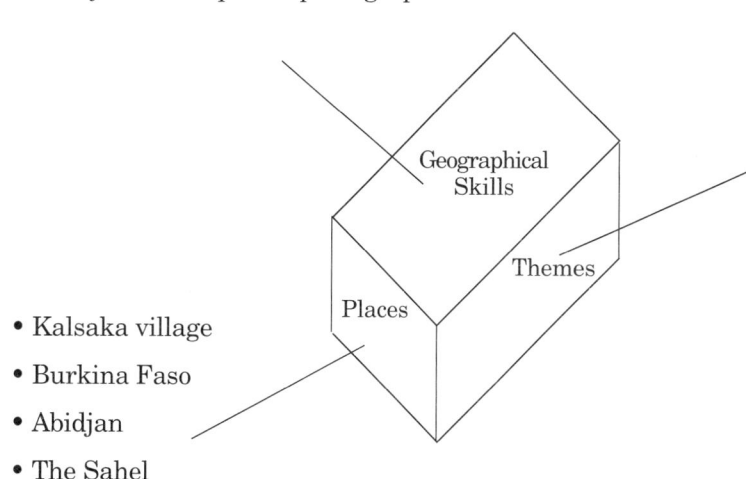

- Kalsaka village
- Burkina Faso
- Abidjan
- The Sahel
- Ivory Coast
- Africa

(Geographical Skills / Places / Themes)

- Human Geography
  - schools
  - food and farming
  - clothes
  - houses and homes
  - irrigation
  - people moving to find work
  - city centres
  - work in cities
  - city life
  - shanty towns

- Physical Geography
  - weather in other parts of the world
  - water supply

- Environmental Geography
  - how fragile environments can be damaged – overgrazing, trampling, collecting firewood, soil erosion
  - how to repair damaged environments

This plan of action can then be related to the pupil record of achievement, as set out on page 93. It is important that children be encouraged to participate in such record keeping, by commenting on specific achievements, and their reaction to aspects of the theme or topic concerned. Only in this way can pupils begin to take real responsibility for their own learning, and begin to set themselves realistic goals. Pupil involvement in negotiating the learning agenda can increase as children become used to identifying their own strengths as well as those areas which require further study. In this way, pupil motivation will be greatly enhanced and levels of achievement raised accordingly.

Important points to remember about assessment

- *Don't panic!* Assessment can take different forms, e.g. mapwork, diagrams, practical activities, discussion. It need not be a test at the end of a piece of work.

- Look on assessment *as part of the planning stage*, i.e. what do you want the children to get out of this unit of work?

- Assessment can be of:
  – groups
  – individuals
  – a whole class

- Some Attainment Targets will be met many times, others may be unique to one topic. There is no need to assess every Attainment Target every time.

- Assessment should record what children can do, not what they cannot.

Assessment, Recording, Cross-curricular elements and Information Technology (IT)

A class record sheet for Key Stage 2

Geography

Names	Attainment Targets														
	AT1			AT2			AT3			AT4			AT5		
	Levels														
	3	4	5	3	4	5	3	4	5	3	4	5	3	4	5

Curriculum mapping

		Level 1 a b c d	Level 2 a b c d e f g h	Level 3 a b c d e f g h i
Geography	Environmental Geography 5			
	Human Geography 4			
	Physical Geography 3			
	Knowledge and Understanding of Places 2			
	Geographical Skills 1			
Tech	Evaluating 4			
	Planning and Making 3			
	Generating Design 2			
	Identifying Needs and Opportunities 1			
Maths	Handling Data 5			
	Shape and Space 4			
	Algebra 3			
	Number 2			
	Using and Applying Mathematics 1			
Science	Physical Processes 4			
	Materials and their Properties 3			
	Life and Living Processes 2			
	Scientific Investigation 1			
English	Writing 5			
	Writing 4			
	Writing 3			
	Reading 2			
	Speaking Listening 1			
	Level 1			
History	The Use of Historical Sources 3			
	Interpretations of History 2			
	Knowledge and Understanding of History 1			

Assessment, Recording, Cross-curricular elements and Information Technology (IT)

Record of Achievement

School _____   Name _____

Topic title _____

Skills   I have used and can describe:

Pictures of people in Burkina Faso and Abidjan.
Pictures taken from the air showing what it is like when the ground dries out.

Places   I have found out and can describe:

About Niftine Sawadogo and her family, and their life in Africa.
About the town of Abidjan.
About the Sahel.

Themes   I have found out, and can describe and explain:

What people's lives are like in a village in Burkina Faso and in the town of Abidjan.
What a woman does during a day.
How the desert is changing people's lives.

The things I need to practise and improve are:

How to use an atlas.
Finding places on maps.

The things I liked best about this topic were:	The things I found hardest in this topic were:
Learning about people in Africa and how they live.	Using an atlas. Explaining why the desert spreads.

Pupil signature

Teacher comment

Record of Achievement

School _____ **Name** _____

Topic title _____

Skills I have used and can describe:

Places I have found out and can describe:

Themes I have found out, and can describe and explain:

The things I need to practise and improve are:

The things I liked best about this topic were:	The things I found hardest in this topic were:
	Pupil signature

Teacher comment

Assessment, Recording, Cross-curricular elements and Information Technology (IT)

Cross-curricular elements

The National Curriculum Council document *The Whole Curriculum* (1990) says: 'Section 1 of the Education Reform Act 1988 (ERA) places a statutory responsibility upon schools to provide a broad and balanced curriculum which:

- promotes the spiritual, moral, cultural, mental and physical development of pupils at the school and of society; and

- prepares pupils for the opportunities, responsibilities and experience of adult life.'

The National Curriculum alone will not provide the necessary breadth, but the ten subjects together with religious education (defined in the Act as the 'basic curriculum') can form the foundation to be augmented by:

- religious education;

- additional subjects beyond the ten subjects of the National Curriculum;

- an accepted range of cross-curricular elements;

- extra-curricular activities.

Cross-curricular elements therefore have to be seen in this context, namely as vehicles which make a major contribution to the development of the child's personal and social education. By definition, cross-curricular elements are not subjects, but they are an integral part of the fabric of all subjects, including geography. The task is to identify where, within the teaching of geographical topics and themes, each of these cross-curricular elements will be encountered, and to this end the NCC has published a series of documents dealing with each element. (These can be obtained from the NCC, Albion Wharf, 25 Skeldergate, York Y01 2XL.)

Cross-curricular elements have three main aspects:

- themes
- dimensions
- skills

Cross-curricular themes

The National Curriculum Council has identified five cross-curricular themes which they recognise as being essential parts of the curriculum. In the sections which follow, examples drawn from Pupil Book 1 and Copymasters 1 are used to illustrate the ways in which *Oliver and Boyd Geography* can assist in teaching cross-curricular themes.

1 Economic and industrial understanding

The aim of education for economic and industrial understanding is to help pupils make decisions about organising their finances and how to spend their money. As a background to this, children need to understand something of how the economic system works and how decisions (by groups and individuals) are made. It also includes references to how economic activity affects the environment and aims to prepare children for their future roles as producers, consumers and citizens in a democracy.

The NCC document, *The Whole Curriculum* (1990), adds 'Education for economic and industrial understanding should cover aspects of industry and the economy'.

The main elements of economic and industrial understanding in *Oliver and Boyd Geography* relate to the work people do (in Pupil Books and Copymasters) and the likely effects of such work on the environment. The following table lists some occupations shown in Pupil Book 1 and Copymasters 1.

Occupations	Unit titles in Pupil Book 1 and Copymasters 1
shopkeeper	A neighbourhood in Inverness (C14, 17, 24)
crossing warden	A neighbourhood in Inverness
factory worker (engineering)	A neighbourhood in Coventry (C22)
quarry worker	Slate from North Wales (C26)
tourist guide	Slate from North Wales
miner	Coal mining in Yorkshire (C36, 37, 39) Slate from North Wales
nurse	Moving to the coast: Southport
farmer/herder	On the move in the Sahel (C51, 52)
various	(C20, 46)

Similarly, the effects of work on the environment are well illustrated in the following units in Book 1:

- *Coal mining in Yorkshire* (effects of opencast and deep mining on the local area).

- *Slate from North Wales* (effects on the environment of quarrying and mining, with its spoil heaps, caves and quarries).

- *On the move in the Sahel* (effects of farming and overgrazing on the environment).

2 Health Education

The emphasis in this theme is on developing ideas relating to a healthy mind within a healthy body. Important elements within health education for children at Key Stage 2 are:

Safety-including the safety of the individual in different environments (e.g. on the way to school, at work, during leisure exercise). In this context the following units of Pupil Book 1 provide references to safety:

Units

A neighbourhood in Inverness   (schoolchildren crossing roads on the way to school)

Slate from North Wales
Coal mining in Yorkshire   (safety is not mentioned directly in these units, but pupils could consider the dangers in past and present mining environments, such as explosions, flooding, etc.)

Assessment, Recording, Cross-curricular elements and Information Technology (IT)

Environmental aspects of health education – the effects on people of e.g. working in unhealthy environments.

Units		*Copymasters*
Slate from North Wales *Coal mining in Yorkshire*	(although not mentioned explicitly in the texts, ideas relating to health education in mining (especially lung diseases) could be developed in relation to these units)	6, 51
Moving to the coast: Southport	(comparisons between unhealthy urban environments (past and present) and coastal environments are made explicitly)	
On the move in the Sahel	(problems of drinking polluted water, and of food shortage)	

Nutrition – the association between diet and health; the nutritional value of foods, and the quality of food preparation and its handling.

Units	
On the move in the Sahel	(problems of malnutrition, need for food aid, etc.)

Health-related exercise – the importance of exercise in promoting good health.

Units		*Copymasters*
Moving to the coast: Southport	(contains many references to out-door leisure activities and facilities)	43, 44, 45, 46, 47.

3 Environmental Education

This cross-curricular theme aims to foster positive and responsible attitudes towards the environment. It is concerned with:

- increasing pupils' knowledge and understanding of the processes (both human and physical) which shape environments;

- helping pupils to recognise the *quality and vulnerability* of environments, e.g. the mountains of North Wales, the Sahel in Burkina Faso;

- helping pupils to identify opportunities for protecting and managing the environment, e.g. irrigation in the Sahel.

Geography has a particularly close relationship with environmental education through Attainment Target 5, Environmental Geography. Here the emphasis is on natural resources, particularly their use and abuse, together with ideas on the fragility of different environments. Linked to these two concepts is the idea of the need to protect and manage particularly valuable and sensitive environments, such as the Amazon Rainforest or Antarctica.

Pupil Book 1 includes three units which deal very specifically with natural resources, and with aspects of environmental management (see page 98).

Units		Copymasters
Coal mining in Yorkshire	(covers coal extraction past and present, and its effects on the landscape)	25, 26, 28 29, 32, 33, 34 35, 38, 42, 49, 50
Slate from North Wales	(includes a section on the uses of slate, as well as its effects on the local environment)	
People on the move in the Sahel	(considers the land as a resource and highlights the consequences of drought and the need for land management, e.g. irrigation)	

4 Education for citizenship

The aims of education for citizenship are:

- to establish the importance of positive, participative citizenship and to provide the motivation to join in;

- to help pupils to acquire and understand essential information on which to base the development of their skills, values and attitudes towards citizenship;

- to foster international understanding. In this context the unit on Burkina Faso is particularly important. It provides the means of raising pupils' awareness of global issues, and enables them to develop skills which will contribute towards an enhanced understanding of world places and issues.

Important elements of education for citizenship which are relevant to Key Stage 2 are:

- community, e.g. the neighbourhood or village (*A neighbourhood in Inverness, A neighbourhood in Coventry, On the move in the Sahel*);

- democracy in action, e.g. cooperation in farming (*On the move in the Sahel*);

- work and employment, (*A neighbourhood in Coventry, Slate from North Wales, On the move in the Sahel*);

- leisure (*Moving to the coast: Southport*).

5 Careers education and guidance

The main aim of careers education and guidance is to help pupils to develop self awareness. Material in Pupil Book 1 and Copymasters 1 (see below) will help teachers to plan activities which will enable pupils to begin this process of self awareness. Much of the material focuses upon the immediate and personally relevant, e.g. journeys to school, local people and the local environment. Such a child-centred approach will enable firm foundations of self awareness to be developed, upon which later careers education will be able to build.

Units	Copymasters
A neighbourhood in Inverness	8, 10, 12, 13,
A neighbourhood in Coventry	20, 46, 47

Cross-curricular dimensions

These include:

- commitment to providing equal opportunities for all pupils;
- preparation for life in a multicultural society.

Oliver and Boyd Geography attempts to foster positive attitudes – through the text, visual material and activities – towards gender equality, cultural diversity and special needs of all kinds. Such approaches permeate the whole series, but particularly useful units in Pupil Book 1 are shown below:

Units	
A neighbourhood in Coventry	(a multi-cultural/mixed community in the UK)
Moving to the coast: Southport	(the special needs of elderly people and how they are met in a typical UK 'retirement town')
On the move in the Sahel	(inequalities in housing, employment, etc. are well illustrated here, especially in the sub-unit on Abidjan).

Cross-curricular skills

These skills (listed below) are transferable, largely independent of content and can be developed in a wide range of different contexts. The core skills are:

- communication
- numeracy
- study
- personal and social
- problem solving
- information technology

These skills are to be found extensively throughout all the materials of *Oliver and Boyd Geography*, but are especially prominent in the tasks and activities developed in the Copymasters.

The Pupil Books in *Oliver and Boyd Geography* will all help to stimulate the use of these skills, and the Copymasters provide activities to develop many of them. In addition, the suggested further activities in Section 2 of this Teacher's Book will help to extend the range of opportunities offered for skills development, particularly in the context of geography.

Information Technology (IT)

Introduction

Information Technology (IT) appears as a fundamental part of the National Curriculum, within Technology as such, and as an integral part of all other subjects.

IT is about more than the acquisition of basic IT skills. It involves applying and developing those skills within a wide range of different contexts-one of which is geography. Indeed, there are many aspects of IT which are best taught in the context of geographical work, and some of these are included in the Statutory Orders for Geography.

Information Technology is concerned with the technology for handling information, especially its storage, processing and transmission in a variety of forms by electronic means. It also concerns the technology used in controlling the operation of machines and other devices. The five strands of IT capability are:

– communicating information

– handling information

– modelling and simulation

– measurement and control

– application and effects

Despite the distinctions between each of these strands, there are also important links and overlaps. As a result it is important that aspects of IT capability are not developed in isolation from each other nor from the rest of the curriculum.

The full development of IT capability involves developing the pupils' ability to:

– feel confident in the use of IT

– identify situations where the use of IT would be appropriate

– select and use IT as appropriate

– evaluate the effectiveness of their use of IT

– understand the implication of IT developments for their lives at home, school and in society.

Many activities will arise out of the use of *Oliver and Boyd Geography* which will provide opportunities for pupils to apply their knowledge of computers, using existing software. Specific ideas for activities are given below, and in the further activities in Section 2 of this Teacher's Book.

Communicating information

IT allows pupils to communicate information as words, numbers, pictures or sounds, to develop, revise and refine their ideas, and to communicate with a range of audiences from class, to school, to neighbourhood.

Types of software (see Appendix 3 for useful addresses)

- word processing
- desk-top publishing
- electronic mail systems
- newsdata systems
- graphics and mapping
- music packages

Activities

1. Children can write descriptions of individual buildings, including houses that they study, and use a computer to produce simple leaflets based on the idea of estate agents' brochures (*A neighbourhood in Inverness, A neighbourhood in Coventry*).

2. During a visit to a quarry or mine pupils can record sights and sounds then use a word processor to write about the visit (*Coal mining in Yorkshire, Slate from North Wales*).

3. Children can use a word processor to describe the area around their school and how it could be improved. After discussion with the teacher they can amend their writing before presenting a final draft.

4. Children can write sentences and paragraphs on a word processor about their thoughts on being trapped in a mine where part of the roof has collapsed (*Coal mining in Yorkshire*).

5. Pictures in Pupil Book 1 can be used to stimulate children to write sentences on the word processor describing what happened before or after the picture was taken (the sub-unit on 'Coventry in the past' is particularly useful here).

6. Data collected from class surveys, fieldwork, Trade Directories etc. (e.g. local shops – past and present – or housing for old people in the area) can be entered on a data base and displayed as graphs. (See *A neighbourhood in Coventry, Moving to the coast: Southport*)

7. Children in an urban locality can exchange survey information with children in a rural locality.

Handling information

IT allows pupils to:

- store, retrieve, modify, process and present material;
- examine patterns and relationships and form and test hypotheses; and
- access information from a range of sources and apply it to learning tasks.

Types of software

- data handling
- spread sheets
- information retrieval
- video text systems
- branching data bases

Activities

1. Maps of routes around the local school neighbourhood can be constructed (similar to the maps in the Inverness and Coventry units in Pupil Book 1).

2. Pictures from the Pupil Book can be used with a word processor to compile questions based on the illustrations, e.g. Where is it? What questions would you ask the people in the picture? What problems do people face in this place? etc.

3   Aerial photographs of the area around the school can be used with overlays on concept keyboards to provide questions and data about the local area.

4   Information collected from fieldwork or from the pictures in the Pupil Book can be entered on to a data base and subsequently interrogated. Some suitable types of data are:

- class methods of travel to school;
- numbers of pupils living in different house types;
- birds/insects/animals seen on a visit to a park;
- building materials used in local houses;
- journey times to local shops;
- numbers of different types of local shops;
- types of goods sold in local shops;
- weather/climate statistics for both local and distant places.

Modelling

IT allows pupils to:

- explore, experiment and create simulations;
- investigate the effect of variables, and so form and test ideas (hypotheses); and
- participate in decisions.

Types of software

- simulations
- adventure programs
- modelling packages
- spreadsheets

Activities

1   Children can use an on-screen picture adventure to explore the rooms of an imaginary house (or the areas of an imaginary garden or park). They can then draw pictures of rooms/the park and make a 3-D model.

2   Following a fieldwork visit to a local canal children can use a program which allows them to operate a lock. They have to consider what happens to water levels as the gates are opened and closed, and they have to navigate a boat through a lock. They have to consider what happens to water levels as the gates are opened and closed, and they have to navigate a boat through a lock.

Measurement and control

IT allows pupils to:

- use computers and microelectronic devices to control and to sense the environment;
- develop problem-solving strategies; and
- begin to understand the working of feedback systems.

IT-based packages

- control software
- programmable toys
- music control systems
- data-logging devices
- satellites and remote sensing

Activities

1 Children can give instructions to a programmable toy to make it turn left, right, etc. and thereby follow a route. (The street maps in *A neighbourhood in Inverness* and *A neighbourhood in Coventry* provide a useful basis for this exercise.)

2 Pupils can give directions to other pupils to guide them through a model street layout, e.g. from home to school or school to shops, using instructions such as left, right, straight ahead (see 1 above for source of examples).

3 During a topic on weather pupils can use a 'mouse' to dress a screen-drawn child with clothes appropriate to the weather. (Examples from *On the move in the Sahel* and *Moving to the coast: Southport*).

Evaluating applications and effects

IT allows pupils to:

- begin to understand the effects of IT on themselves, their families and the community;
- understand some advantages and disadvantages of IT;
- reflect on their own use of IT;
- begin to understand that electronically-stored data are not always accurate; and
- begin to understand the implications of storing personal information electronically.

Activities

1 Children can talk about appliances at home or school and list the ways in which equipment responds to switches and signals, e.g. video, automatic kettles.

2 Groups of children can draw and paint a range of toys which they are able to control. They can also discuss the countries in which such toys are made and the materials from which they are constructed.

3 Children can draw and paint street furniture which responds to switches and signals, e.g. traffic lights, street lights, railway crossings, telephones. Photographs and drawings in Pupil Book 1 can be used to identify these different examples.

A list of addresses for IT Support and Software is given in Appendix 3.

Note: The ideas in the above section on IT are developed from *School-Focused Development Materials for Key Stages 1, 2 and 3*, published by NCET (1991), ISBN 1 85 3791164.

Section 5:

Implementing National Curriculum Geography at Key Stage 2: developing school - based INSET

Introduction

The purpose of this section is to provide some prompts and ideas to help teachers prepare themselves for implementing the Statutory Orders for geography at Key Stage 2. Reference to the *Oliver and Boyd Geography* materials is made throughout and it is recommended that teachers familiarise themselves with all the published components before starting an INSET session. In particular, it will be helpful to have read Sections 1, 2, 3, and 4 of this book.

It is assumed that most schools will be in the same position as they approach the start of a National Curriculum programme in geography:

- a member of staff will have been designated the role of geography co-ordinator;
- many staff will not be geography specialists and may be concerned about their own level of geographical knowledge, as well as about how to interpret and implement the Statutory Orders;
- all staff are under pressure, and time for curriculum planning is at a premium.

The key purpose of an INSET session for geography is to help all staff to achieve the following objectives:

- to find out what geography involves at Key Stage 2.
- to identify which elements of geography they are already covering in their existing programmes;
- to adapt existing work, and plan future work, in order to fulfil the requirements of the Statutory Orders;
- to establish a means of evaluating, assessing and recording pupils' progress in geography;
- to collect together the resources needed for teaching and learning about geography (see Section 1 of this book, and the Appendices).

The role of the geography co-ordinator

The co-ordinator is faced with a formidable range of tasks, some of which are set out below. It is hoped that *Oliver and Boyd Geography* will provide support for the co-ordinator, both as a source of essential background information and as a means of implementing a school programme which they can confidently assume will meet the requirements of the Statutory Orders.

> **The main tasks of the geography co-ordinator**
>
> 1. To provide advice and guidance to other staff.
> 2. To produce guidelines, a scheme of work and other planning documents.
> 3. To update and maintain resources, including IT.
> 4. To support other staff in respect of background knowledge or skills (e.g. map reading).
> 5. To monitor the teaching and learning of geography in the school.
> 6. To evaluate, keep records and assess.
> 7. To organise INSET.
> 8. To co-ordinate geographical work with work in other subjects.
> 9. To liaise with other schools, other phases and the LEA or other advisory groups.

Planning school-based INSET: some key questions

What is the main purpose of this INSET session?

To raise awareness of the geography Statutory Orders.

To evaluate published resources.

To carry out an audit of current practice.

Remember: limited objectives make for more productive INSET sessions.

Which staff will be involved in the INSET?

Will it be all staff or only those involved in Key Stage 2?

How long will the session last?

In what ways will the staff be actively involved in the session?

Examples: evaluating assessment sheets

selecting suitable stories from which to extract geographical ideas.

Do all staff understand the purpose and objectives of the session?

What is the intended outcome of the INSET session?

Examples: a list of resources to be purchased in this financial year

a whole school policy for geography.

Clearly, some outcomes, such as a whole school policy, will require several INSET sessions over a period of time, whilst others (e.g. deciding on IT resources) will take much less time.

Managing curriculum change

There are three main questions to discuss regarding the introduction of National Curriculum geography into the school:

1. Where are we now?
2. Where do we want to be?
3. How are we going to achieve what we want?

Where are we now?

Staff, with the help of the co-ordinator, can carry out an audit of present practice, the main aim being to highlight geographical work already covered in the existing schemes. (A list of Statements of Attainment for levels 3, 4 and 5 and the Programme of Study for Key Stage 2 can be matched against present schemes.)

Other things to consider during the audit process are:

Resources	What do we use?
Time allocation	How much time is currently devoted to work which can be called geographical?
Curriculum content	What curriculum areas are currently covered in thematic work? Note which Statements of Attainment are covered by existing work.
Assessment	How is work currently assessed? Is there a geographical element in assessment? (Refer to Section 4 in this Teacher's Book for guidance and ideas on assessment)
Teacher expertise and confidence	How confident do teachers feel about dealing with topics which have a geographical content?

In some schools such an audit may highlight important areas of concern. For instance, the staff may conclude 'we don't seem to do any geography'. Don't panic! Once starting points are understood real progress can be made.

Where do we want to be?

What is geography and what does it mean for children at Key Stage 2?

The NCC's Non-statutory Guidance document defines geography as follows:

'Geography is concerned with the study of *places*, the human and physical processes which shape them and the people who live in them. It helps pupils make sense of their surroundings and the wider world.' (See Section 3 of this Teacher's Book for a detailed breakdown of the Statutory Orders).

What are our aims and objectives for the teaching of geography at Key Stage 2 in this school?

(See Section 3 of this book.)

Do we need a school policy document on geographical work?

If so, who will write it, and what sections will it have? (Refer to this Teacher's Book for ideas.)

What is the nature of the match between our present practice and the Statutory Orders for geography?

In particular, how far do we cover the content and how far do we encourage the enquiry approach? (See Section 3 of this book.)

How appropriate are our present resources for National Curriculum Geography?

(Refer to *Oliver and Boyd Geography* Pupil Books, Copymasters and Sections 1, 2, 3 and 4 and the Appendices of this Teacher's Book.)

How are we going to achieve what we want?

Resources Consider which current resources (including IT) can be redeployed and which additional ones will be required. Also consider which will be needed first and which later so that expenditure can be phased over several terms or years.

School debate Staff will need to consider other general issues, such as:

- How much time should be allocated to work with a geographical content?

- What are the most appropriate methods of delivering the geography National Curriculum? (See NCC and CCW Non-statutory Guidance documents and this Teacher's Book.)

- Will additional funds be needed for published resources, fieldwork, computers, etc?

- What are staff needs, e.g. INSET, background information on the National Curriculum requirements? (See this book, Section 3.)

Planning a Key Stage 2 programme

One approach, outlined below, describes a sequence of activities which highlight:

- current work with a geographical component

- additional geographical work required in future year(s).

This could form the basis of a staff INSET session relating the existing situation to future requirements.

Planning for Key Stage 2

Outline the existing programme of topics and themes for Key Stage 2, in the school, identifying content and skills covered.

⬇

Identify the geography content in the existing programme.

⬇

Match the existing geographical content with the Programmes of Study for both Key Stage 1 and Key Stage 2. Look for overlap.

⬇

```
┌─────────────────────────────────────────────────────────────┐
│ Identify geographical knowledge, skills, places and themes   │
│ not already covered.                                         │
└─────────────────────────────────────────────────────────────┘
                              ⬇
┌─────────────────────────────────────────────────────────────┐
│ Discuss how far the 'missing' geographical elements can/     │
│ should be incorporated in themes and topics currently taught │
│ and decide if new themes and topics need to be added to the  │
│ programme.                                                   │
└─────────────────────────────────────────────────────────────┘
                              ⬇
┌─────────────────────────────────────────────────────────────┐
│ Decide which type of topic is most appropriate in each year  │
│ in order to deliver the geographical knowledge, skills, and  │
│ ideas required by the Statutory Orders. E.g. a geographically│
│-focused topic on 'mining' or a more broadly-focused topic on │
│ 'transport'.                                                 │
└─────────────────────────────────────────────────────────────┘
                              ⬇
┌─────────────────────────────────────────────────────────────┐
│ Produce an outline which describes the broad geographical    │
│ content for each term of each year for Key Stage 2.          │
└─────────────────────────────────────────────────────────────┘
                              ⬇
┌─────────────────────────────────────────────────────────────┐
│ It is important not to plan each key stage in isolation, so  │
│ reference must be made to Key Stage 2 themes and topics.     │
│ This will ensure that the content is organised so that       │
│ children's progression may be identified in terms of:        │
│                                                              │
│ - a widening scale of study                                  │
│                                                              │
│ - returning to key ideas at higher levels                    │
│                                                              │
│ - introducing greater precision                              │
│                                                              │
│ - developing and refining skills.                            │
└─────────────────────────────────────────────────────────────┘
                              ⬇
┌─────────────────────────────────────────────────────────────┐
│ Check the new themes and topics against both Attainment      │
│ Targets and the Programme of Study to ensure complete        │
│ coverage. (See matrix on page 15 in this book.)              │
└─────────────────────────────────────────────────────────────┘
                              ⬇
┌─────────────────────────────────────────────────────────────┐
│ Explain the new outline of themes and topics to colleagues   │
│ who can then refine it.                                      │
└─────────────────────────────────────────────────────────────┘
```

Planning a unit of work based on key questions

A sample plan is given on page 111. It shows how the resources of *Oliver and Boyd Geography* can be used to teach the topic of *People on the Move* in a coherent way.

It addition it suggests how assessment ideas can be incorporated into the planning process.

Staff could carry out a similar activity for either their current topic, or a future one, using the blank planning sheet on page 110.

Implementing National Curriculum Geography at Key Stage 2

Key Stage 2 Year 3/4	Unit title: On the move		Time allowed: half a term	
Key Questions	Activities	Resources from O & B Geography	Statements of Attainment	Assessment
1 What things move?	• Brainstorm things which move – people, animals, plants, goods (large, small, heavy, valuable, perishable)	Slate from North Wales	AT4/3c	Copymaster 31
2 How are things moved?	• For road, rail, air, water, list advantages and disadvantages of each (e.g. fast/slow; carries large/small loads).	Coal mining in Yorkshire		
3 How do we choose the right transport?	• Decision-making activity relating different types of goods (e.g. lettuce, fresh flowers, coal, timber, slate, diamonds) to each type of transport			
4 What are the reasons for movement, and what types of movement do people make?	• Brainstorm types of and reasons for moves, e.g. to go shopping, to go to work, to visit relatives, to move home	Moving to the coast: Southport	AT4/3a	Copymasters 43, 44, 45, 46, 47
5 Why do people move house?	• Provide case studies of families describing why they moved (e.g. change of job, retirement, need for larger/smaller house, desire to live in different neighbourhood)			
6 How do people choose the places to which they retire?	• Use atlases, maps, publicity material from places etc. for children to compare the advantages of different places (e.g. on the coast, lots of retirement flats, plenty to do etc.)			**Possible Assessment Focus** List reasons why people move house (see Copymaster 43).
7 What are retirement places/towns like?	• Use maps, photographs etc. to study Southport in detail. Look at the facilities/activities for retired people in the town.			

Key Stage	Unit title:			Time allowed:	
Key Questions	Activities	Resources from O & B Geography	Statements of Attainment	Assessment

Assessment in geography

For INSET purposes, the sub-section in this book on 'Assessing and recording pupil progress' (pages 88-94) should provide useful guidelines. In addition, the following Assessment checklist provides one example of the way in which children's work can be assessed, and so serves as a starting point for discussion of issues such as:

- What are the most suitable types of assessment?
- What elements should be included in assessment for geography? (places, themes, skills)
- Which pupil activities lend themselves to assessment?
- What school-based assessment items should be produced?
- Should the school produce its own assessment guide?

Within *Oliver and Boyd Geography*, the Copymasters provide ready-made assessment items, many of which can be used in association with an existing school programme to test pupils' grasp of geographical skills. Others link more closely with the Pupil Books and so provide a means of assessing the pupils' understanding of the key ideas in those books, as well as developing geographical and cross-curricular skills. (See the Copymaster matrix on pages 16, 17 of this Teacher's Book, and the sections on the Copymasters, pages 9, 11.)

Assessment checklist

The following checklist highlights selected elements of the geography Attainment Targets in order to help teachers make statements about individual pupil progress. For simplicity, the subject can be broken down into these three components:

Skills   – use of maps

              – compass bearings

Areas   – home locality

              – localities in the UK and the world

Themes   – weather

              – places to live (settlements)

The following list is **very selective**, giving only sample indicators of level for each component. Teachers may wish to devise their own list.

Skills   – *mapwork*

              Level 3:   able to use the eight points of the compass

              Level 4:   able to use four-figure grid references

              Level 5:   able to use six-figure grid references

       – *routes*

              Level 3:   able to construct a simple route

              Level 4:   draw a sketch map using symbols and a key

              Level 5:   able to follow a route on a 1:50,000 OS map and describe the features which would be seen

Areas — *home locality*

- Level 3: describe and explain activities in the home locality
- Level 4: describe the geographical features of the home region
- Level 5: describe how the characteristics of the home region are interrelated

— *other localities*

- Level 3: identify and compare features and activities in a contrasting UK locality and in another locality outside the UK
- Level 4: describe how daily life in an economically developing country is affected by weather, landscape and wealth
- Level 5: explain how the occupations, land use and settlements of a locality outside the UK are related to environment and location

Themes — *weather*

- Level 3: describe weather which is typical of contrasting localities outside the UK
- Level 4: describe how site conditions can influence surface temperatures, and local wind speed and direction
- Level 5: distinguish between weather and climate

— *settlements*

- Level 3: identify evidence indicating the reasons for those settlements
- Level 4: describe the layout and function of a small settlement or part of a large settlement
- Level 5: analyse the factors that influence the location and growth of individual settlements and identify the effects of such growth.

Fieldwork in Geography at Key Stage 2

Fieldwork is central to all geographical enquiry, as the Programme of Study for Key Stage 2 makes clear: 'Enquiry should form an important part of pupils' work in Key Stage 2. It should take account of pupils' interests, experience and capabilities, and lead to investigations based on fieldwork and classroom activities.'

Fieldwork is one important means by which teachers can make geography *real* to their pupils. For example, visits to local shops to investigate parking problems, or surveys to discover whether men are worse litter louts than women, will linger in the child's memory long after more abstract ideas have faded. It is important to remember that fieldwork need not involve long journeys to coastal or mountain (or desert!) areas. First-hand investigation of the environment local to the school is more than adequate, and is less expensive and less disruptive of the whole school timetable.

Fieldwork should be seen as a process rather than as an event. It needs careful preparation and planning, together with the all-important follow-up. The process might be seen as a flow diagram:

Decide on aims and methods of fieldwork, i.e. what are we investigating and why?

⬇

Discuss fieldwork with children and encourage their input. Get them to identify key questions to be asked, and problems to be investigated. All children should be actively involved.

⬇

Carry out all preliminary tasks, e.g. informing school, parents, governors, local police; taking out insurance; visiting site of fieldwork; identifying key sites; briefing helpers.

⬇

Discuss problems to be investigated and children's ideas of possible solutions, together with information needed to resolve such problems. Then discuss best methods to collect information.

⬇

Collect information on field visit.

⬇

Process the information into usable form, e.g. graphs, maps and sketches which relate to the problems under consideration.

⬇

Evaluate original problem. Were original ideas good ones in the light of the fieldwork? Do we need to change our ideas? What new ideas for study have we discovered? Did we solve the problem we started with?

A number of ideas for local fieldwork are included under the 'Further activities' heading within Section 2 of this book. These relate to the key topics, skills and ideas developed in Pupil Book 1. This Pupil Book, and the ten *Oliver and Boyd Geography* titles for key Stage 1, also provide stimuli and starting points for local fieldwork – in particular, the locality studies such as *A neighbourhood in Inverness,* and *A neighbourhood in Coventry* in Pupil Book 1. The maps and photographs in these units could be compared with similar resources collected for the neighbourhood of the school, and tasks similar to those in both Book 1 and the related Copymasters 1 could be used to guide pupils in their own local investigations.

Appendices

Appendix 1

Geography resource check list

1 *Books*
   Text books
   Teachers' handbooks
   Atlases
   Children's reference books
   Story books

2 *Non-book resources*
   Maps - Ordnance Survey (see Appendix 4)
   Globes - maps - other
   Photographs
   Aerial photographs
   Pictures
   Playmats
   Games
   Weather recording instruments
   Compasses
   Wall charts
   Wall maps
   Newspaper articles
   Directories (including telephone)

3 *People*
   The children
   Parents, grandparents
   Shopkeepers, etc

4 *The local area*
   Houses, shops, parks
   Farms, fields
   Streams, ponds

5 *Collections*
    Topic collections from Schools Library Service

    Development Education Centres

    Postcards, posters

    Artefacts

    Pictures

    Brochures

    Labels from food

6 *School resources*
    Local maps

    School in contrasting area

    School in economically developing country

7 *Organisations*
    Geographical Association

    Christian Aid, Action-Aid, Oxfam, etc.

    Schools Library Service

8 *Publications*
    Primary Geographer (GA)

    Junior Education

    Child Education

    National Geographic Magazine

    Philip's New Geographical Digest

9 *Audio-visual*
    Slides, videos

    Schools broadcasts

    Commercial videos

    Camera

    Computer software

Appendix 2

The books listed here are all suitable for use with children at the start of Key Stage 2 and have been selected because they include material which relates to geography.

Ahlberg J & A *Jeremiah in the Dark Woods* Fontana-Lions

Bond R *The Cherry Tree* Gazelle/Hamish Hamilton

Bond R *The Eyes of the Eagle* Blackbird Books/Julia MacRae Books

Bond R *Flames in the Forest* Blackbird Books/Julia MacRae Books

Cherrington C *Sunshine Island Moonshine Baby* Fontana Young Lions

Crebbin J *Ride to the Rescue* Puffin

Foreman M *Dinosaurs and all that Rubbish* Picture Puffins

Forsyth A *The Monster Flower Show* Gazelle/Hamish Hamilton

Furminger J *Nicholas and the Brilliant Idea* Gazelle/Hamish Hamilton

Gardam J *Kit in Boots* Puffin

Gardam J *Bridget & William and Horse* Macmillan Education

Grey N *A Balloon for Grandad* Orchard Books/Oliver & Boyd

Hartley D *Up North in Winter* Macdonald

Hedderwick M *Katie Morag Delivers the Mail* The Bodley Head

Hendry D *Hetty's First Fling* Redwing/Julia MacRae Books

Joy M *The Little Explorer* Viking Kestrel

Joy M *The Little Lighthouse Keeper* Puffin

Karusa trans. Elkin J *Nowhere to Play* A & C Black

Kent L *Seasonal Norm* Gazelle/Hamish Hamilton

Kingman L *The Meeting Post* Redwing/Julia MacRae Books

Kipling R *Just So Stories*

Krasilovsky P *The Cow Who Fell in the Canal* Puffin

Nash M *The Haunted Canal* Viking

Nimmon J *The Red Secret* Antelope/Hamish Hamilton

Peyton K *Going Home* Oxford University Press

Pullein-Thompson C *Runaway Ben* Gazelle/Hamish Hamilton

Sampson F *Jenny and the Wreckers* Antelope/Hamish Hamilton

Stevens C *Anna, Grandpa and the Big Storm* Puffin

Swindells R *The Ice Palace* Fontana Lion

Waddell M *Going West* Picture Puffin

Paton Walsh J *Babylon* Beaver Books

Wildsmith B *Professor Noah's Spaceship* Cape

Poetry

Hull R *Autumn/Winter/Spring/Summer* (4 books) Wayland

Waters F *Out of the Blue* Lions/Collins

Appendix 3

Useful addresses

The following list shows some of the main suppliers of software appropriate for primary school work.

GSN Software Ltd
(Technical support for KEY)
50 Stamford Street
Ashton-under-Lyme
OL6 6QH
(061 339 6635)

Information Education Ltd
Enterprise Centre
Bedford Street
Stoke-on-Trent
ST1 4PZ
(0782 281643)

ITV Association
6 Paul Street
London
EC2A 4JH

KEYDATA
Longman Resources Unit
62 Hallfield Road
Layerthorpe
York
YO3 7XQ
(0904 425444)

KITE Software
139 Finstall Road
Finstall
Bromsgrove
B60 3DE
(0527 78898)

NCET (materials)
Hoddle, Doyle and Meadows
Old Mead Road
Elsenham
Bishops Stortford
CM22 6JM
(0279 813939)

NCET (publications)
Sir William Lyons Road
Science Park
University of Warwick
Coventry
CV4 7EZ
(0203 416994)

Science Education Software
Unit 12
Marian Industrial Estate
Dolgellau
Gwynedd
LL40 1UU
(0341 423305)

SPA Ltd
PO Box 59
Leamington Spa
CV31 3QA

Appendix 4

Useful addresses (Geographical resources and support)

The following organisations all provide a range of materials and support appropriate for teaching geography in primary schools, including publications for pupils and teachers; journals; posters. The Geographical Association has a primary school section and special journal, *Primary Geographer*, which contains many useful teaching ideas and resources.

Centre for Global Education
York University
York
Y01 5DD

Centre for World Development
Education
Regent's College
Inner Circle
Regent's Park
London
NW1 4NS

Commonwealth Institute
Kensington High Street
London
W8 6NQ

The Council for Environmental
Education
School of Education
University of Reading
London Road
Reading
RE1 5AQ

Development Education Centre
Selly Oak Colleges
Bristol Road
Birmingham

Friends of the Earth
26-28 Underwood Street
London
N1 8LL
(There may be a local branch in your area.)

The Geographical Association
343 Fulwood Road
Sheffield
S10 3BP
(There may be a local branch in your area.)

National Association for
Environmental Education
West Midlands College of Higher
Education
Gorway
Walsall
WS1 3BD

National Trust Education Manager
36 Queen Anne's Gate
London
SW14 9AS

Ordnance Survey
Romney Road
Maybush
Southampton
S09 4DH

Oxfam
274 Banbury Road
Oxford
OX2 7DZ

Royal Society for the Protection of
Birds (RSPB)
The Lodge
Sandy
Bedfordshire
SG19 2DL
(There will be a regional branch near you.)

World Wide Fund for Nature
Panda House
11-13 Ockford Road
Godalming
Surrey